Wired and Mobilizing

Routledge Studies in Science, Technology and Society

Wired and Mobilizing

Social Movements, New Technology, and Electoral Politics

Victoria Carty

Routledge
Taylor & Francis Group
New York   London

First published 2011
by Routledge
270 Madison Avenue, New York, NY 10016

Simultaneously published in the UK
by Routledge
2 Park Square, Milton Park, Abingdon, Oxon OX14 4RN

Routledge is an imprint of the Taylor & Francis Group, an informa business

© 2011 Taylor & Francis

Typeset in Sabon by IBT Global.
Printed and bound in the United States of America on acid-free paper by IBT Global.

Library of Congress Cataloging-in-Publication Data
Carty, Victoria.
    Wired and mobilizing : social movements, new technology, and electoral politics / by Victoria Carty.
        p. cm. — (Routledge studies in science, technology and society ; 13)
    Includes bibliographical references and index.
  1. Social movements—Technological innovations.   2. Internet in political campaigns.   3. Internet—Social aspects.   4. Online social networks—Political aspects.   5. Social media—Political aspects.   I. Title.
    HM881.C367 2011
    322.4'40973—dc22
    2010011745

ISBN13: 978-0-415-88070-1 (hbk)
ISBN13: 978-0-203-84276-8 (ebk)

Contents

Acknowledgment

Thank you, Miguel, for your inspiration and helping me to understand the true treasures and blessings of life. Thanks to the countless peers, friends, and colleagues who have always supported me. And most importantly, thank you mom and dad, for everything.

Introduction

There has been a proliferation of research on social movements during the past several decades, and the emergence of new information communication technologies (ICTs) and the digital media boom have strongly affected this scholarship. Electronic social movement organizations (SMOs) and online activists are redefining political struggle across the dimensions of contentious and electoral politics in terms of recruitment, mobilizing and strategizing, fundraising, and campaigning. Not only have SMOs gone online to disseminate information and publicize protest information, but the explosion of e-movements, e-protest, and e-activism highlights the importance of the Internet as an organizational tool (Earl and Schussman 2003). Wired activism has become a significant, if not essential, repertoire for social movement actors within the new communication landscape which allows activists to engage in new forms of disruptive activity (such as hacktivism and e-mail spamming), and/or adapt existing modes of contention to an online environment (virtual sit-ins, online petitions, etc.).

As Castells (2007) notes, historically, communication and information have been fundamental sources of power and counter-power of domination and social change. He summarizes: "Indeed, the ongoing transformation of communication technology in the digital age extends the reach of communication media to all domains of social life in a network that is at the same time global and local, generic and customized in an ever-changing pattern. As a result, power relations . . . as well as the processes challenging institutionalized power relations are increasingly shaped and decided in the communication field" (p. 239). Additionally, new digital technologies and the World Wide Web allow for more varieties of group formation and support among individuals, even the most transient sectors who care about similar issues, as like-minded people are easier to find in cyberspace (Brecher, Costello and Smith 2009).

Since the mid 1990s we have witnessed a number of struggles in which marginalized groups have used the Internet to create or sustain mobilizations. For example, it was through the Internet that a worldwide movement developed to challenge the neoliberal agenda proposed by the OECD (Organization of Economic Co-Operation and Development) in 1995. The treaty put forth was the Multilateral Agreement of Investment which sought to liberalize cross-border investment and trade restrictions, and would have greatly expanded the role of investors at the expense of national governments, workers, and the environment. However, it was leaked over the Internet by non-governmental organizations and disseminated over various listserves which led to international protest and criticism (Kobrin 1998). This was one of the first instances of activists using electronic communication to engage in direct civic communication outside of traditional broadcast media and national elites.

A few years later, the 2001 "Battle of Seattle," which successfully shut down the World Trade Organization meetings (in large part because the local police force and public officials were completely caught off guard), was perhaps the first major example of the significance of the Internet in terms of the intersection between online and offline mobilizing. The Internet and other forms of technology facilitated and coordinated not only the various networks of global protesters, but also permitted an international division of labor prior to and during the protests (Van Aelst 2002). Leading up to the three-day protest, in which over 500,000 activists from all over the world participated, actions were electronically organized and mobilized via e-mail, bulletin boards, chat rooms, cell phones, and alternative media outlets. Previous to the protests activists created the IMC (Independent Media Center), a worldwide network of Internet activist sites that serves as both news media and a forum for grassroots mobilization under the umbrella of Indymedia (Kidd 2003). This enabled the rapid dissemination of text images, video, audio, and regular updates about the situation as it unraveled in real time. The Center was designed so that anyone could post information directly online without moderation or limitation, and set the model for a many-to-many use of the media whereby activists can subvert the traditional one-to-many approach under mainstream and corporate media. There are now over 130 Indymedia websites that are constantly activated for local and global protests.

The World Wide Web and Indymedia also facilitated global and simultaneous protests to coincide with the Seattle protests. Demonstrations were held in over eighty locations in dozens of countries (Rheingold 2002). These were organized through the Website (http://www.seattlewto.org/N30), which put out action alerts and calls for action in ten different languages to provide information regarding how potential participants could contact local directors all over the world. These protests set a pattern that was followed by demonstrations in nearly every major summit over the next few years that targeted powerful economic/political entities, proposed treaties, regulatory agencies, and trading blocks. This included the International Monetary Fund, The World Trade Organization, the World Bank, the Free Trade Treaty of the Americas, EU meetings, and the G8 summits among others (Kahn and Kellner 2004).

In a perhaps more intriguing case, the potential of ICTs was also illustrated in 2004 by the Zapatistas in the remote and desperately poor region of Chiapas, Mexico. They had declared war on the Mexican government on January 1, 2004 to coincide with the signing of the North American Free Trade Agreement (NAFTA). They used the Internet, e-mail, listserves, and various websites to reach an international audience who mobilized to pressure the Mexican government to adhere to a ceasefire. The EZLN (Zapatista National Liberation Army), however, worked through *mediated* relationships. They did not have access to the Internet or computers, but would hand off written materials that were prepared as communiqués for the mass media to reporters or supporters (mainly Canadian and U.S. activists) to be given to reporters. These then were typed and/or scanned for distribution over the Internet (Arquilla and Ronfeldt 1996). The EZLN also assembled widespread supporters in two intercontinental meetings to promote its sovereignty from the Mexican government and contest NAFTA. The first was held in Chiapas in 1996 and the second in Spain the following year. Thousands attended from over forty countries and five contents and what was to be discussed, the agenda, and the logistical arrangements were all done over e-mail (Cleaver 1998).

More recently, protests following the 2009 Iranian presidential election against alleged electoral fraud regarding the victory of Ahmadinejad's reelection (and in support of opposition candidate Mir Hossein Mousai) demonstrated the power of not just the Web but also social networking sites. The mobilization was in fact nicknamed the "Twitter Revolution" and the mobilization highlighted two things. One, that digital tools have altered communication into something much more "real-time" than the Internet. And two, the use of new technologies among activist has decreased or eliminated the need for any kind of formalized or centralized leadership in many contemporary social movements. As the Iranian government limited press operations, restricted journalists, blocked access to pro-opposition Websites, shut down Internet access, blocked cell phone transmissions and text messaging, and banned rallies in response to the protests, it was Twitter, Facebook, and YouTube that allowed the mobilization to sustain itself (Santana 2009). The catalyst for the uprising was when Neda Agha-Soltan, a young female Iranian was shot and killed by police during a protest. Amateur videos of the episode and her death spread virally across the Internet after being posted to Facebook and YouTube, and were eventually picked up by mainstream media coverage. This sparked solidarity among Iranians abroad in the United States, Britain, and Canada who protested outside of Iranian embassies in Washington, DC, London, and Toronto in solidarity (Albawaba 2009). Not to be outdone by the activists' ingenuity, the Iranian government posted false information that Moussavi had conceded the election and called off the protests. However, the digital community, realizing the posting was from a government agent, used Twitter and blogs to form an e-movement. They also called on users to change their personal information and time-zone settings to make it appear that they lived in Iran to foil attempts to track bloggers by time-zone searches (Albawaba 2009).

In each of the above instances marginalized and oppressed groups were able to mobilize and gain support from others by circulating information via alternative media and new digital technologies. However, it must be noted that these technologies are certainly not monopolized by progressive social movement actors, and that the Internet has both democratic and anti-democratic potentials. Conservative and extremist groups use the Internet, Twitter, MySpace, YouTube, and Facebook in similar ways. The demonstrations against health-care reform and the Tea Parties that challenge the Obama administration's attempt at reform, as well as the use of the Internet to increase recruitment for jihad groups or the Ku Klux Kan, clearly demonstrate this. Also, as will be noted in the following chapter, the Internet can be used to allow for new modes of surveillance in attempts to penetrate the mediums used by citizen activists.

Whereas it is necessary to acknowledge that the Internet and social networking sites are not partial to any political orientation or group, this book does focus on progressive social movements and electoral politics by examining four diverse cases of civic engagement and mobilization. The goals of this manuscript are to (1) examine case studies of movement dynamics in a variety of empirically-based settings; (2) develop the conceptual foundations and theoretical frameworks for analyzing social movements that go beyond previous analyses; and (3) advance our understanding of how ICTs are affecting contentious politics, civil society processes, and institutional politics. To explore not just the *how*, but also the *why* of social movements, I anchor each of these case studies in an encompassing theoretical framework to examine the conditions for the emergence, context, participation and recruitment, dynamics, and consequences of collective behavior. Typically, scholars have approached case studies grounded in a particular literature or from a single theoretical model. These often fail to recognize the connections between apparently dissimilar works, narrow the focus of social movement research, limit the applicability to other forms of collective behavior, lead to a certain degree of fragmentation, and result in partial perspectives.

To account for these shortcomings this book attempts to illuminate what I view as some of the overlapping concepts and theories by using an approach that is interdisciplinary—embracing theories from political science, sociology, and communication studies. It explores the interconnected dimensions of social movement phenomena to yield a more comprehensive, unified, and holistic theoretical model and generalizable framework, even if not a complete theory, that can help future researchers to assess the impact of contentious and electoral politics on policy. I do not perceive the various perspectives that have been applied to social movements as mutually exclusive or competing. Nor do I privilege one perspective over the other. Rather, I include both cultural and political dimensions of collective behavior and integrate the various theoretical perspectives to examine the values, modes, constructs, and process at work behind both disruptive and institutional forms of collective behavior. I devote attention, both theoretically and empirically, to how resource mobilization, political process, and cultural theories that include framing analysis and new social movements interact and shed light on different aspects of the character and dynamics of social movements.

Perhaps the main contribution of this research is to push the literature forward to include the importance of the Internet. Previous theoretical models as applied to collective behavior do not present a right fit for much of the contemporary mobilization occurring online or using online technologies. Also, much of the work on ICT influences on movement practices comes from practitioners, journalists, and communication scholars who place the role of ICTs analytically first. From a sociological standpoint, I ground each analysis within a framework of social and political dynamics that drive the usage of new technologies as related to social movements.

The first chapter summarizes the various theoretical frameworks of social movement studies to highlight the strengths and weakness of each, and suggests that for the field to advance a more integrative approach is useful. I also update the extant literature by examining how the Internet and other ICTs have affected the potential for political organizing. Chapter 2 analyzes the Students against Sweatshops Campaign (USAS), with a special focus on Nike Corporation in the struggle for corporate social responsibility regarding labor practices. It also includes an examination of how the Culture Jammers movement targeted not only Nike's labor abuses, but also the contradictory messages between the images associated with Nike products through its advertising campaigns and the exploitation of its workers. The third chapter focuses on the revitalization of the peace movement following the 9–11 attacks in the United States and the subsequent war on terrorism which ultimately led to a coalition of the "unwilling."

Whereas each case study in this text acknowledges the role of both contentious and institutional politics, the cases in chapters four and five lean more toward the institutional side of the spectrum. Although over the past several years both social movement studies and political science have cast aside the rigid distinctions between the domains of social movements, interest groups, and electoral politics, we can't disregard the boundaries all together. MoveOn.org, one of the most successful public policy advocacy groups in the United States, is a great example of how the digital era allows political advocacy groups to gain leverage both within and outside of the formal political Party structure. It also raises questions about the relationship between social movements and political institutions, as well as how some organizations that are part blogoshpere/part concrete are affecting social change offline and online. The last case study focuses almost exclusively on social change within the formal political arena in an analysis of the 2008 presidential election. It outlines how ICTs have revolutionized the way candidates campaign, with a particular focus on Barack Obama's ability to tap into the youth vote given their high levels of engagement with the

Internet, and more importantly, the activation of social networking sites. The core themes running through each case study in Chapters 2 through 5 are the application of social movement theory to explain why/how each of these phenomena took place, and also the critical role that ICTs played. Whereas the first three lend themselves to celebratory conclusions regarding how new technologies can enhance grassroots mobilization to empower marginalized citizens, the Obama campaign (and to a lesser extent MoveOn) illustrates something quite different. I caution that before we idealize the technological revolution brought about by the Internet and new forms of digital technology, we must be aware of the continuity between old and new forms of communication and how elite power are still able to manipulate and control the new communication environment.

Admittedly, there are some limitations to this work. Although two of the four case studies (USAS and the peace movement) are international in scope, the focus is largely on dynamics within the United States. The other two, which focus more on the relationship between grassroots activism and electoral politics, are situated explicitly within the United States. Thus, both the analytical approach and focus is by and large U.S.-centric. However, despite this, the research does fill a gap in the area of academic research, and I believe that the conceptual and theoretical trajectory as applied to each study allows for a springboard for examination inside as well as outside of the United States. The data are drawn from a variety of sources including scholarly sources, the mainstream and alternative press, organizational documents, and the World Wide Web. For the purposes of this book I was not sampling documents per se but for looking materials that could help clarify the emergence, developments, and dynamics of the contemporary social movements under scrutiny that then could be analyzed within the rubric of social movement theory.

ACKNOWLEDGMENT

Portions of Chapter 3 appeared in *International Journal of Peace Studies* and are reprinted in this volume with permission of the journal editor. Portions of Chapter 4 appeared in *Research in Social Movements, Conflict and Change* and appear in this volume with permission of the journal editor.

1 Overview of Social Movement Theories and a Proposed Synthesis

Over the past several decades political scientists and sociologists have offered a variety of theories and empirical research to enhance our understanding of collective behavior. The focus of political science has been primarily on the relations between social movements and political parties, and the function of social movements in relation to agenda setting and influence on the polity (Chapters 5 and 6 will address these dynamics in detail). The main emphasis within sociology has been an attempt to explain the emergence and timing of social movements, the social and political context in which they develop, recruitment efforts, the mobilization of resources, and outcomes/consequences of collective behavior. Recently, sociologists, as well scholars of communication studies, have added to the literature by exploring how new information communication technologies (ICTs), such as the Internet and other forms of digital media, are being used to organize and mobilize activists across a host of issues at both the global and local level. There is general consent among social movement theorists that this latter development requires new theoretical examination.

This chapter provides an overview of the main theoretical frameworks that have been employed by researchers to explain the dynamics of social movements. These include traditional theories of collective behavior, resource mobilization, political process, and cultural-oriented perspectives such as framing and "new" social movement theory. I briefly provide an overview, or summary, to highlight the strengths and weaknesses of each. I do articulate on the various perspectives in more depth in the following chapters as they are applied to specific case studies. This chapter also urges those of us who study social movements to cease from focusing on one particular theory to explain a specific phenomenon, and to move in the direction of a synthesis, integrating the various perspectives which are too often viewed as distant approaches. By analyzing the various perspectives as complimentary rather than as competing, or privileging one over the other, I hope to advance the field of social movement studies by offering a more integrative model that will hopefully prove fruitful for future empirical research.

TRADITIONAL THEORIES OF COLLECTIVE BEHAVIOR

Early theories of collective behavior explained social movements through a micro-level lens rooted in social psychology. Sociologists during the first half of the twentieth century viewed social movements as random occurrences, deviant-based, and emotionally-charged responses among aggrieved individuals to unsatisfactory situations and conditions. For example, structural strain and relative deprivation theories argued that social movements emerged among individuals who felt deprived of some goods or resources, and/or experienced a sense of inequality in relation to others or to their expectations (Morrison 1978; Smelsner 1962). The overall motivating factors and explanatory variables were perceived to be grievances. Also underlying these theories was the "mass society" proposition which suggested that movement participants consisted of those who were not fully integrated into society, and thus collective behavior provided a sense of belonging to a larger group (Gusfield 1962, 1970; Kornhauser 1959; Blumer 1939).

These psychologically-based theories have largely been rejected by contemporary scholars of social movements (although certain strands of social movement theory have begun to reincorporate the role of emotion, in conjunction with other factors, to help explain collective behavior). McAdam (1982) in particular provides a critique of the classical model of collective behavior. He argues that the claim that social movements are a response to social strain or relative deprivation is problematic because it ignores the larger context in which movements arise, and thus the political dimension of collective behavior. He further contends that identifying individual discontent as the most significant cause of social movements cannot adequately explain how discontent translates into collective phenomena. Because most people feel deprived on some level at some point in time, these theories cannot explain why some individuals and groups mobilize and others don't. The reasoning is also circular in that the evidence for deprivation is the movement itself (Jenkins and Perrow 1977). Additionally, an assessment of the mobilization of external and internal resources, recruitment efforts, cultural explanations, and outcomes of collective behavior were largely ignored by the classical model.

Beginning in the 1970s the perspective of collective behavior began to change considerably. Terms like "mass society" are no longer used to explain social movements, and have been replaced with conceptualizations of social movement activists as rational actors. According to more recent theories, social movements are broadly defined as a collective challenge by a plurality of actors with a common purpose and shared conflictual issues who work in solidarity through sustained interactions to articulate resistance to elite opponents and authorities (Tarrow 1994). Tilly (2004) suggests that there are three main elements to social movements: campaigns (sustained, organized public efforts making collective claims on target authorities); repertoires (tactics that a group has at its disposal given a certain socio-political environment); and WUNC (worthiness, unity, numbers, and commitment). Key to any social movement are mobilizing strategies—"those collective vehicles, informal as well as formal, through which people mobilize and engage in collective action" (McAdam, McCarthy, and Zald 1996:3).

Topical literature also addresses social movement outcomes and explanations as to why social movements succeed or fail (Soule and Olzak 2004; Burstein and Linton 2002; Giungi, McAdam, and Tilly 1999; Frey, Dietz, and Kalof 1992). Although no direct causal relationship can be categorically established between collective behavior and success, many have suggested that variables such as taking strategic advantage of existing political opportunities (Meyer and Minkoff 2004; Suh 2001; Kitschelt 1986; Tarrow 1986); the tactics that social movement actors employ (Tilly 2006; McAdam 1983); expressing a clearly defined set of goals that movement supporters can relate to (Jasper 1997; Zald 1996; Benford 1993; Snow et al. 1986); access to resources and forming alliances that expand the movement's base of support (Gamson 1990; McCarthy and Zald 1977; Olson 1971); and the organizational forms and practices social movement actors adopt (Ganz 2004; Gamson 1990; Staggenborg 1988; Piven and Cloward 1977) play a critical role.

More specifically, some scholars maintain that successful outcomes occur either when the challengers' goals are realized or when the target of collective action recognizes the challengers as legitimate representatives of a constituency, thereby altering the relationship between the challengers and target (Marullo and Meyer 2004). Others also note that consequences do not just entail clear cut victories or failures in the institutional political arena (Jenkins and Form 2006; Amenta and Young 1999). Rather, cultural variables such as changes in values and public opinion, the establishment of collective identity and/or subcultures, and new cultural opportunities are also significant in terms of social movement outcomes (Polletta 2008; Earl 2004; Williams 2004; Johnston and Klandermans 1995; Buechler 1993).

RESOURCE MOBILIZATION

Whereas earlier assessments of collective behavior viewed social moments as deviant aberrations, the resource mobilization paradigm argues that social movements are formed by rational social actors and social movement organizations (SMOs) that undertake strategic political action (Buechler 1999; Morris 1984; Jenkins 1983; Olson 1971). This perspective ascertains that social movements develop when individuals with grievances are able to mobilize sufficient resources that included external and internal support. It therefore focuses on organizational dynamics and specifically on how individuals, groups, and organizations access and utilize resources (McCarthy and Zald 1987, 1973; Tilly 1978; Oberschall 1973). These resources include knowledge, money, media attention, labor, solidarity, organizational structure, legitimacy, and support from political elites. Participants are characterized as purposeful and motivated on the basis of a calculation of the costs and benefits regarding participation. This in turn is influenced by the presence of resources and available networks among SMOs (Gamson 1975; Tilly 1975; McCarthy and Zald 1973).

One of the main drawbacks of resource mobilization is that to large extent it ignores the external political context at the macro level. Another shortcoming is that it tends to emphasize instrumental action oriented toward political participation while paying little attention to the cultural and symbolic dimension of social life that often underpins such strategic action (Habermas 1987, 1984). Critics also challenge that its lack of focus on collective identity undermines its ability to explain social movement strategies, activities, and motivation to participate. Because individual participation is explained by a cost/benefit analysis of resources, non-strategic reasons, and cultural dynamics such as grievances rooted in emotion and mechanisms for social solidarity or collective identity of groups are excluded as explanatory variables (Polletta and Jasper 2001; Jasper 1997). In many current social movements, for example, there is little or no material gain on the part of individuals who join. For example, without compassion, indignation, and moral shock the transnational moments against sweatshops, the war against Iraq, support for the Zapatistas and Iranian protestors would have been narrower and less able to recruit people. Furthermore, its heavy focus on social movement organizations is problematic in that many contemporary social movements do not have a traditional organizational structure, but can better be characterized as decentralized "social movement communities" that operate in an ad hoc fashion (Wollenberg et al. 2006; Polleta and Jasper 2001; Staggenborg 1998; Buechler 1993).

POLITICAL PROCESS THEORY

The political process model suggests that movements are vastly affected by resources *external* to social movement actors—political opportunities structures—and shifts attention toward the relationship between institutional political actors and protest. Like resource mobilization, it represents an alternative to the classical (psychological) model by viewing social movements first and foremost as political phenomena (Tilly 1973), and therefore agents can only be understood in the broader context of political opportunities. Also similar to resource mobilization, this theory assumes rational choice on the part of protesters, who evaluate their political environment and make calculations about the likely impact of their collective action (Gamson and Meyer 1996). The political context therefore affects mobilizing efforts and influences which claims will be pursued, which alliances are likely to ferment, and which political strategies and tactics will be chosen (Amenta and Caren 2004; Kresi 2004; Kitschelt 1986; McAdam 1982).

On the other hand, going beyond resource mobilization as well as classical theories of collective behavior, this perspective argues that some groups may have an insurgent consciousness and resources to mobilize, but because political opportunities are not open, they will not have any success. Hence, each of the three components are requisites for lucrative mobilization efforts and for social movements to be influential as those with shared grievances must be able to convert a favorable structure of political opportunities into an organized and mobilized campaign of social protest (McAdam 1982). Political opportunities refer to a few things. One is the receptivity or vulnerability of the existing political system to challenge (Meyer 2005; Tarrow 2001). This vulnerability can be the result of one or a combination of any of the following: a decline in repression (and thus increased tolerance for protest), fragmentation among political elites, electoral instability, broadening access to institutional participation, and support of organized opposition by elites (Tarrow 1996; Jenkins and Perrow 1977; Piven and Cloward 1977; Gamson 1975).

The importance of the last variable, having allies in positions of power in the polity, has been substantiated in several studies (see Meyer and Staggenborg 1996; Tarrow 1994; Gamson 1990; Jenkins and Perrow 1977). Another key element, as noted, is division among elites. This allows groups to manipulate the competition between powerful members of the polity, and for social movement actors to take advantage of openings that result from these struggles (Tarrow 1994). The subsequent shifts within the institutional realm of politics improve the chances for successful social protest by reducing the power discrepancy between insurgent groups and their opponents (Meyer and Minkoff 2004). McAdam (1982) argues that *either* undermining the structural basis of the political system, or enhancing the strategic position of insurgent challengers is beneficial because both result in an increase in the political leverage exercised by challengers.

Although political process theory fills an important void in the literature by focusing on institutional dynamics of social movements, there are a few caveats. The diversity of the approaches of using political process theory has led to confusion because often the same terms and variables are used to describe a variety of different factors (Meyer and Minkoff 2004; McAdam 1996). For better clarification, these scholars argue that there is a need to distinguish between general openness in the polity and openness to particular constituencies (issue-specific opportunities), between formal institutional and more informal structures of power relations, and a broader understanding of the relationships among institutional politics, protest, and policy.

Another drawback is that the theory presupposes that all aspects of social movements—their emergence, dynamics, cognition of participants and their susceptibility to join political protest, and outcomes—are determined by macro structural relations (Goodwin et al. 2001; Gamson and Meyer 1996). A focus on structural opportunities without considering the cognitive processes which intervene between structure and action can be misleading. Activists' perception of available opportunities and the lenses through which they view potential opportunities for their moments, i.e., their subjective perceptions of reality and interpretive frameworks, are significant to understanding their efforts.

To address this last criticism and refine the political process model scholars have introduced what they call the political mediation model (McAdam 2005; Tarrow 1998; Gamson and Meyer 1996). This paradigm examines the way in which the social and political context that participants are situated in intersects with the strategic choices that social movement actors make and recognizes that opportunities are indeed situational, fluid, and volatile because they depend on the way actors *perceive* and *define* the situation, and then decide what action should be taken.

A final critique, that has yet to be rectified, is that the availability of political opportunities are typically relevant only to dissatisfied citizens striving for moderate and mainstream institutional political change within a two-party democratic system. Similarly, social movements operating outside of civil society cannot be accounted for as these types of opportunities are not significant to the mobilization of countercultural and identity-based movements (whose primary goals are not political), or to movements that seek radical, systemic change (Kriesi et al. 1995).

FRAMING ANALYSIS, COLLECTIVE IDENTITY, AND NEW SOCIAL MOVEMENTS

Both resource mobilization and political process theories have been criticized for paying little attention to the cultural dimension of social movements, the role of collective identity, and the use of collective action frames as employed by SMOs (Goodwin et al. 2001; Gamson and Meyer 1996; Klandermans 1991; Klandermans and Tarrow 1988). Besides the availability of political opportunities and resources, there are other mitigating factors that can help explain the emergence of social movements, reasons for participation, and the strategic choices that social movement actors make. To acknowledge these shortcomings, those working within the tradition of resource mobilization, and later those writing on "new" social movements, have begun to embrace aspects of social constructionism.

The "cultural turn" within more contemporary literature focuses mainly on the *why* (the meaning of collective action and subjective interests), rather than on the *how* of social movements (political conditions and resources available). Many have called for a new social psychology that can more accurately depict how framing, politics, ideology, emotions, and values help to create and sustain a sense of collective identity and motivate people into action (Polletta and Jasper 2001; Jasper 1997; Klandermans 1997; Melucci 1996). Research within this tradition asserts that actors are not merely utility-maximizers, but are often immersed in rich normative commitments as a result of close ties to other individuals, groups, traditions, and broader ethical or moral sentiments. In contrast to the cost/benefit basis of whether or not individuals decide to mobilize, recent studies suggest that often there is an immaterial quality that motivates individuals which is rooted in collective identity. As argued by Polleta and Jasper (2001), collective identity can be a *perception* of a shared status or relationship, which may be imagined rather than experienced directly. By appealing to identity, social movements motivate participants through intrinsic rewards such as self-realization personal satisfaction, and providing a sense of group belonging (Gamson 1992).

Melucci (1996) defines collective identity as an interactive, shared process that links individuals or groups to a social movement through sustained interaction. It is constructed and continually negotiated, and provides a shared cognitive worldview. This is different from "mobilizing interests" as conceptualized by traditional resource mobilization theory because it is a constructivist concept, illuminating how individuals come to decide they share certain orientations and grievances and decide to act collectively (Polletta and Jasper 2001; Snow and McAdam 2000). A concentration on collective identity therefore compliments previous theories by helping to bridge the gap between the structural foundations for action and the collective action itself. In other words, collective identity serves as an intermediate level of analysis in that it links the "how" and "why" of collective behavior.

Key to forging collective identity and articulating shared meanings is the way organizers "frame" their issues to resonate with potential recruits. They do this by linking participants' grievances to mainstream beliefs and values to mobilize and maintain solidarity (Taylor and Van Dyke 2004; Diani 1996; Benford 1993; Gamson and Wolsfield 1993; Snow and Benford 1992; Snow 1986). Specifically, a frame is defined as an interpretive schema that an individual or group uses to interpret reality, on an ideologically basis, by selectively omitting and emphasizing various aspects of the world (Snow 1986). Within social movement theory frames are typically referred to as "injustice frames" that contain implicit or explicit appeals to moral principles (Ryan and Gamson 2006; White 1999; Benford and Hunt 1992; Snow and Benfrod 1988).

For framing to be influential organizers must persuade large numbers of people that the issues they care about are urgent, that alternatives are possible, that there is a worthiness (or moral standing) of the activists, and that the constituencies they seek to mobilize can be invested with agency (Tarrow and Tilly 2006). As expressed by Snow et al. (1986), social movement actors must provide "prognostic," "diagnostic," and "motivation" frames. This means identifying problems (including attributions of blame or causality so that the movement has a target for its actions), posing solutions in a way that mobilizes participants and appeals to third parties, and stimulating a "call to arms" by encouraging people to take action to solve a given social problem.

Other concepts employed by framing theorists include "frame align-ment," which is a process through which individual interests, values, and beliefs are articulated as congruent and complimentary with SMO activi-ties, goals, and ideology (Snow et al. 1986). "Frame bridging" involves the ability of SMOs to reach people who already share their political orienta-tion through consciousness raising efforts and organizational outreach, thus enlarging the boundaries of an initial frame to include issues or social prob-lems of importance to potential participants. And finally, "frame amplifi-cation" appeals to deeply held values and beliefs in the general population and links those values and beliefs to movement issues (Snow et al. 1986).

"New" social movement theory also borrows from the literature on framing and collective identity to help clarify the intermediate steps from condition to collective action. The more politically-oriented branch of NSM theory conceptualize changes in identity formation among social movement actors as manifestations of macro-level social and economic changes in postindustrial societies. NSMs are viewed as a reaction to colo-nizing intrusions of states and markets, and are grounded in the resistance of the professional middle class to the rationalizing forces of modernity, social fragmentation, injustices, and the politicalization of everyday life (Johnston et al. 1994; Mouffe 1992; Habermas 1987; Touraine 1985). Offe (1985) suggests that the emergence of NSMs must be understood as a reac-tion against the deepening of what he perceives to be the irreversibility of forms of domination in late capitalist societies and the global nature of many social problems, which in turn, is bringing forth a convergence of multiclass- and multi-identity-based struggles.

Following this theme, Giddens (1991) summarizes: "The system of late modernity, on an individual and collective level, has radically altered the existential parameters of social activity. It is a politics of self-actualization in a reflexively ordered environment, where that reflexivity links self and body to systems of global scope. . . . Life politics concerns political issues which flow from processes of self-actualization in post-traditional contexts, where globalizing influences intrude deeply into the reflexive project of the self, and conversely where processes of self-realization include global strat-egies" (49). He further argues that the age of late modernity has allowed the development of a "post scarcity economy" in which basic survival needs are met for most people, and subsequently allows them to focus on issues outside of class.

Others theories within the NSM paradigm reflect more exclusively on the cultural domain. They identify forms of domination in semiotic terms and emphasize the decentralized nature of power and resistance. Within this tradition scholars center on everyday life and cultural and symbolic forms of resistance, and argue that this occurs alongside or in place of more conventional political forms of contestation (Cohen 1985). New actors, whose identity is flexible, fragmented, and shifting do not seek control, power, or economic gain. Instead, the struggle is oriented toward control over the process of meaning, autonomy, creativity of relationships, and ways of defining and interpreting reality (Castells 2001; Rucht 1988; Habermas 1981; Melucci 1980). By eschewing strategic questions and instrumental action in favor of symbolic expressions of resistance, the goal is often cultural and personal change, and actors are more concerned with retaining or recreating endangered lifestyles and culture than with changes in the economic or public policy realm. Some explicitly argue that the field of social conflict has shifted from the political sphere to civil society and the cultural realm because it is in these areas where new collective identities and forms of solidarity are being established (Offe 1987; Tourraine 1985; Melluci 1985).

Although different scholars focus on different themes, within the NSM literature there is increasing agreement that the "newness" is a quality both of the social structures to which movements respond and the forms of collective action and mobilizing strategies (Johnston 1994). There is also consensus among most theorists that the newness is to distinguish certain forms of collective action and identity from those based exclusively on class-based interests and Marxist reductionism (Mouffe 1992; Laclau and Moufe 1985).

In essence, NSMs refer to a diverse array of collective actors who are raising new issues, are the carriers of new values, operate in new terrains, employ new modes of action, and have presumably displaced the old social movements of proletarian revolution (Cohen 1985). It is also widely recognized that the organizational features of contemporary social movements are distinct from traditional forms of organization (for example labor unions or political parties) because they are constituted by loosely articulated, decentralized, and egalitarian networks (Castells 1997; Gusfield 1994; Mueller 1994; Melucci 1989).

Whereas this perspective has proven valuable in revisiting the role of culture and emphasizing the importance of struggles reflected in civil society, there are certain shortcomings as well. As summarized by Tarrow (1991), the supposed "newness" of social movements overstates their novelty, ignores their organizational forerunners and long-term historical cycles of cultural critique, confuses an early position in a cycle of protest with a new type of protest, and misinterprets contemporary phenomena as a qualitative shift in collective action. In support of these criticisms, most theorists concede that there is more continuity in terms of representation, organizational structures, and social movement actors' relationship with political institutions than the categorization of new social movements implies (Johnston et al. 1994; Larana 1994). Additionally, the often exclusive focus on the cultural aspects of contemporary movements and the assertion that civil society is the only arena for collective action precludes an analysis of the political dimension of social movements (Cohen 1983). Many contemporary social movements are much more than cultural phenomena; they are also struggles for institutional reform. An over-emphasis on identity furthermore lends itself to ignoring questions of strategy and a discussion of *how* identity develops in the process of interaction. A final weakness is that the specific organizational dimension of social movements (organizational dynamics, leadership, recruitment, tactics, and resources that enable or constrain SMOs) is often overlooked.

THEORIES OF NEW INFORMATION COMMUNICATIONS TECHNOLOGIES

Theories of newly emerging ICTs, and particularly those of the Internet, resonate with NSM theory and critical theory because both pay attention to the significance of democratic discourse in modern societies and how the recent "technological revolution" is affecting forms of communication and mobilization efforts. Because information has become a crucial resource in postindustrial societies, collective action designed to change the ways in which public discourse is structured is of great significance (Castells 2001; Harvey 1998). Newly emerging ICTs, that in many ways are used and experienced differently from conventional media and information systems, have the potential to redefine social relations, cultural practices, and economic and political orders. Habermas (1993, 1989), one of the leading critical theorists and advocates of NSM theory, has argued that it is the tendency in advanced capitalism for political economy arrangements to dominate and colonize the communicative life world that is prompting new forms of social resistance to revitalize democracy. Media consolidation, he observes, has served as a corrosive social force by denying citizens a voice in public affairs while at the same time enhancing the power of corporate interests. Public opinion is now administered by political, economic, and media elites who mediate public opinion as part of social control. However, NSMs, viewed as struggles in defense of the public sphere (the space that mediates between the private sphere and the sphere of public authority), provide a way for citizens to regain forms of communicative action and participatory democracy (Habermas 1983).

To explore this trend further, Castells (2001, 1997) refers to the processes of what he calls the "network society." He argues that the Internet may be the most persuasive and effective form of communication technology in diffusing social ideas and actions in history, and claims it is now an integral part of the very fabric of social life because of its ability to distribute information and power. This invigorates a new type of "informational politics" in which electronic media become the space of politics by framing processes, messages, and outcomes and results in a new kind of civil society based on "electronic grassrooting of democracy." Social agency, he proposes, is now expressed through practices of identity politics because the diffusion of new ICTs has prompted the development of horizontal networks of interactive communication via a many-to-many flow of communication. The Internet can serve as a medium through which collective identity is established and sustained because it enhances the visibility and marketability of opinions and opportunities, and in contrast to the one-to-many mass communication media citizens comment on, and/or pass along information they receive (Jenkins 2006; Van Aelst and Walgrave 2003; Diani 2000; Kollock and Smith 1999; Pliskin and Romm 1997).

Similar utopian perspectives regarding ICTs can be found in the sociology and communication studies literature. Poster (1995), for example, argues that the recent technological advances have "enabled a system of multiple producers, distributors and consumers to use decentralized and newly accessible media technologies in everyday practices . . . this electronically mediated communication can challenge systems of domination" (28, 57). Kidd (2003) espouses that ICTs offer a mode of communication that is fundamentally resistant to state regulation, reducing a state's capacity for repression by hindering its ability to control the flow of information and political communication. Within the institutional political realm new forms of organizational flexibility and efficiency among online groups provided by ICTs increases their ability to influence policy processes by subverting the "professional" campaign model and dominant media corporations, thus giving rise to a new type of civic engagement at the grassroots level (Bennett and Iyengar 2008; Jenkins 2006; Langman 2005; Kellner 2004). Many also credit the Net for allowing for the development of community in spite of physical distance as it is not bounded by political borders or identities—enabling new forms of virtual community and political formulations. These "virtual public spheres" of the Internet facilitate what Kahn and Kellner (2003) call "post-subcultures." These are interpersonal networks of discussion, debate, and clarification that, although virtual, do indeed foster/create spaces for the democratic construction, negotiation, and articulation of new constellations of identities to act both locally and globally. These networks of interpersonal ties are indeed "real" in terms of forming durable relations that provide a number of social rewards including sociability, identity, and support networks.

In the same way, others contend that computer mediated forms of communication allow for democratizing processes of collective action and political organizing by flattening bureaucratic structures and making boundaries more permeable (Carty 2010; Bennett et al. 2009; Best and Krueger 2006; Pasek et al. 2006; Bimber 2003). This in turn facilitates collaborative decision-making, coalition-formation among organizations, lowers the obstacles to grass-roots mobilization and organization, and speeds the flow of politics. Bimber (2003) refers to these attributes to new communication and information flows as "accelerated pluralism." This represents a shift toward a more fluid, issue-based group politics. Research also shows how digital network configurations can facilitate permanent campaigns and the growth of broad networks despite relatively weak social identity and ideology ties (Brecher, Costello and Smith 2009; Nip 2004; Bennett

2003; Rheingold 2003; Van Aelst and Walgrave 2003). Jenkins (2006) uses the term "civic media" to describe how new electronic mediums can foster face-to-face civic engagement and participatory culture, often referred to as the "spillover" effect. And lastly, Dutta-Bergman's (2006) research suggests that individuals living in communities with Internet access are more likely to be involved in local community organizations than those living in non-access communities.

A more critical analysis of electronic mediated information systems, however, reveals a number of limitations. Some claim that virtual social relations in cyberspace are not a substitute for more traditional forms of community, protest, and collective identity due to a lack of interpersonal ties that provide the basis for the consistency of collective identities and ability to mobilize new members (Putnam 2000; Kraut et al. 1998; Pickerill 2003). Underlying this concern is an ongoing discussion about whether new forms of media and technology are weakening or strengthening standard forms of political and social engagement (see Bimber 2003; Putnam 2000; Kraut et al. 1998). Many discussion groups and listserves also discourage challenges to the information and conclusions drawn by members because they tend to be composed of like-minded people who are often predisposed to issues that draw Internet users to various sites (Jordan 2001; Diani 2000). Also, citizens tend to seek out what information they think will be relevant to them. As Bimber and Davis (2003) claim, the Internet is "par excellence" the medium for eliciting selectivity.

Other critiques of the Internet note the elite domination over cyberspace and control over listserves by list owners or gatekeepers, and problems regarding access to technology or the digital divide (Dimaggio et al. 2004). In the political sphere, Howard (2006) observes that despite grassroots efforts, political elites are still very much a part of the political campaign process. He suggests that new computerized forms of communication are used to create "managed citizens"—meaning that political managers are using digital media not merely to collect public opinion, but also to create it. As citizens interests are represented through data profiles, some of which is generated knowingly and some of which is collected without informed consent. Furthermore, challenging some of the more optimistic assessments regarding use of the Internet among youth, initial research suggested that high levels of Internet use were linked to social isolation from family and community, and were associated with higher levels of depression (Nie 2001; Nie and Erbring 2000; Kraut et al. 1998). However, these findings have been disputed on several accounts (see a follow up study by Kraut 2002 as well as Wellman 2001; Guest and Wierzbricki 1999; and Wuthnow 1998).

Despite the pros and cons of new digital technology and communication systems, there is ample evidence that the Internet has resulted in a significant shift in communication capacity and potential for political organizing. It has dramatically changed the way information is sent, received and accessed. However, there remains a certain level of continuity with traditional forms of mainstream and conventional forms of media and communication, and there is still leverage for elite control over new technologies (Lievouw and Livingstone 2006).

A SYNTHESIS

Over time, each theoretical model that addresses social movements, supported by empirical research, has advanced the discussion of collective behavior. Resource mobilization compliments the explanatory power of the political process model by acknowledging that it is the resources available, shared among internal and external social movement actors and SMOs, that facilitate insurgent groups' ability to exploit political opportunities. Political process theory adds to resource mobilization by highlighting that even if the resources are available, the political context can support or hinder mobilization efforts. However, many current forms of mobilization cannot be explained only by the political context of the internal/external resources and therefore these perspectives must carefully consider the formation of collective identities, framing processes, and the role of culture in explaining the "why" of social movements. New social movement theory and the framing perspective call our attention to the fact that collective action emerges not necessarily because of objective conditions or resources available, but because of how the actors identify such conditions which is often a result of framing processes and collective identities.

Thus, a more useful approach may be a genuinely interdisciplinary one (although avoiding much of the fragmentation in the extant literature) and one that acknowledges that there is a political, socio-historical, and cultural context to any social movement. Such a paradigm is acutely aware of the complex interplay of macro-, meso-, and micro-level dynamics and addresses both the "how" and "why" of collective behavior. It also recognizes that because most contemporary social movements (as well as political campaigns) use the Internet, theories of how new ICTs impact political struggle are essential to most, if not all, discussions of collective behavior and social change. Additionally, to avoid the confusion of theoretical categorizations such as "new" social movements (which tend to understate the commonality of collective behavior over the past several decades), and of the overstatement of ICTS "revolutionizing" communication and mobilization efforts, a more cautious approach is cognizant of continuities between contemporary and past forms of collective behavior, as well as between traditional communication outlets via mass media and new media platforms. The nuanced method that I apply to each case study in the following chapters is guided by looking at the social movement or political campaign at hand, and analyzing it in terms of how each theory adds explanatory power to the emergence, formation, dynamics, characteristics, and outcomes of the mobilization.

2 Students Against Sweatshops and Corporate Social Responsibility
The Anti-Nike Campaign

Contemporary economic globalization, which is driven and regulated primarily by multinational corporations (MNCs), has a direct impact on workers' lives. International decentralized subcontracting arrangements allow MNCs to constantly relocate production in the pursuit of lower wages and lax labor laws, leading to what is referred to as the "race to the bottom" and sweatshop conditions. The low-wage and/or politically repressed working classes in developing countries allow capitalist enterprises to both reduce their labor costs and control the work force through the constant threat of relocation (Gereffi and Korzeniewicz 1990). Additionally, outsourcing alleviates MNCs' responsibility for the working conditions.

The combination of a fear of jeopardizing their jobs, ignorance, extreme poverty, and relatively closed political opportunity structures is so great in most developing countries that workers are often reluctant, if not powerless, to press for their legal rights. Although unfair and illegal business practices by MNCs are not a recent phenomenon, typically in the past companies were not exposed of partaking in them because of the spatial and cognitive separation between production and consumption. Over the past decade, however, interest about sweatshop labor has rapidly increased and consumers have begun to question where their merchandise comes from, under what conditions it was assembled, and who did the work and for what pay. And these questions are impacting purchasing decisions. According to a survey conducted by Marymount University in 1999, 86% of consumers said they would be willing to pay extra to ensure that their clothing was not made in sweatshops (marymount.edu). In that same year, PIPA survey data recorded that 74% of consumers agree that "if people in other countries are making products that we use, this creates a moral obligation for us to make efforts to ensure that they do not have to work in harsh conditions," and 75% said they would be "willing to pay $25 instead of $20 for a piece of clothing that is certified as not having been made in a sweatshop" (PIPA 1999).

This chapter examines ways in which activists, on a local and global level, have organized against the race to bottom, and focuses specifically on Nike Corporation, which is one of the most visible targets of the anti-sweatshop campaign. It highlights that although the power and autonomy of MNCs have increased under accelerated processes of globalization, we are also witnessing novel modes of grassroots organizing solidified through globalized resistance to exploitative tendencies driven by the race to the bottom.

Although Nike experienced tremendous growth between the early 1970s and mid 1990s, dominating the global athletic footwear and apparel market, in the late 1990s it began facing fierce criticism for its use of cheap overseas labor, and what many deemed as hypocritical marketing and advertising campaigns. As a result (although there were likely other contributing factors such as the downturn of the Asian economy), in 1998 Nike revenues and stock price dipped by nearly 50% and the company was forced to lay off 1,600 workers (Egan 1998). Due to pressure from workers, activists, and consumers it was eventually forced to take responsibility for working conditions in its outsourced factories.

One of the groups most active in the mobilization was USAS (United Students Against Sweatshops). It organized in 1998 to establish codes of conduct that corporations holding licensing agreements with various universities were mandated to follow. Additionally, the international Culture Jammers movement played a key role in exposing the contradictory images between Nike's advertising/marketing messages and its business practices. To contextualize this case study I employ theories of political process, resource mobilization, framing, and new social movements (in addition to select strands of postmodern theory that examine links between political economy and the cultural and media industries). Together, these perspectives offer a framework that illustrates how marginal groups are able to develop micro-level forms of resistance to challenge macro-level structures and trends.

GLOBALIZATION, POSTMODERNISM, AND NEW SOCIAL MOVEMENTS

The contemporary era can be characterized as one undergoing an intensified process of globalization, understood in terms of economic, political, cultural, and technological change (Dicken 1998; Poster 1995; Giddens 1990; Castells 1989). Accompanying this is a qualitative change in the degree of international interdependence, consciousness, and interaction throughout the world. Some theorists refer to this era as "postmodernism" or "postmodernity." There is much debate and confusion surrounding these concepts, but in a very general sense, I am focusing on the discourse of postmodernism that refers to a response to socioeconomic developments impacted by global and consumer capitalism, technological advances, and the increasing relevance of advertising and the media in contemporary society (see Bauman 1997; Best and Kellner 1991; Harvey

1989; Baudrillard 1988; Jameson 1984). These scholars argue that the new economic order is one based on flexible labor markets, products, and patterns of consumption fueled by quickly changing fashions as articulated through new sign systems and imagery. As images become central to social life, the realm of marketing, advertising, and the media become integral to cultural and economic activities. Jameson describes postmodernism as the "cultural logic of late capitalism," with the central focus being on the expanding commodification emerging from mass consumption and mass culture.

There are competing views as to whether human agency is stifled or invigorated under these new economic, cultural, social, and technological developments. Some have adopted a technological deterministic perspective. Baudrillard (1988), for example, conceives the postmodern era to be one of sheer simulations and claims that because consumer goods are sold as symbols and they form their own kind of reality, and thus the economic system is now based on the "hyper-reality of floating values" (41). He concludes that the subject has lost the ability to dominate the object due to a triumph of effect over cause and surface over depth. Because power has become completely abstract, operating merely through the circulation of signs, which are devoid of meaning. Therefore, forms of domination are immune to rationalist critique as traditional forms of political strategy are undermined.

Jameson also views the role of human agency hindered by the hyper-consumption of signs and images and the accompanying commercialization of social life. However, unlike Baudrillard, he has not given up on political struggle. He concedes that social relationships become dislocated under enhanced processes of globalization and the symbiosis between media and the market, and the political ramifications are that people become less aware of the structures that shape their lives. In order to combat consumer capitalism, according to Jameson, individuals must become aware of their individual and collective sense as subjects in multinational capitalism on a social as well as a spatial scale—what he labels a "radical politics for now" (301).

Following Jameson's lead, others (Best and Kellner 1997; Haraway 1991; Habermas 1987) also contend that through the process of deconstruction and targeting forces of decentered power, the diffusion of resistance politicizes new areas of social and personal experience, such as lifestyle choices. Thus, the potential for social change under postmodern conditions, according to their assessment, is best anchored in the formation of coalitions based on affinity, contingency and mobile positioning, or what Haraway suggests as "using what is shared in common at a particular time and setting" (71). Postmodernity, in sum, offers a reflexivity or self-consciousness and creates new possibilities for social relations in a wide variety of sectors (economic, political, and social), condoning a more pluralistic form of activism that is based on articulations among flexible sources of identity.

New Social Movements

There is some substantial overlap between theorists of postmodernism and scholars working within the NSM paradigm. As noted in Chapter 1, NSMs are distinguished from previous social movements that were based primarily on economic concerns and material gain. They embody diverse coalitions whose mission is to make issues such as equity, dignity, and well-being as important as capital accumulation (Evans 2000; Sklair 1998). Tomlinson (1999) describes NSMs as those based on "distanciated identity," whereby individuals embrace a sense of what unites us as human beings, of common risks and possibilities, and of mutual responsibility (194). They are indicative of an increased consciousness that embraces a global, compassionate perspective, and practice a type of political strategy termed "globalization from below" in order to modify the institutional forms of organized globalization from above. This involves grassroots activities across disperse geographical locations, and identity politics (in a global formation) is seen as the most fruitful way of resisting all forms of injustices within the global system.

This agenda also resonates with the ideology of cosmopolitanism as promoted by Beck (2006), Hahn (1987), and Mellucci (1996). Similar to much of the NSM literature, cosmopolitanism is concerned with micro-level dynamics (lifestyle choices) as well as macro-level or structural components at the global and institutional level. For example, Hahn offers the concept of "Interbeing" which refers to a way of living one's life in relation to others on a local and global scale that is based on compassion and understanding. Beck stresses the potential for the formation of global citizens' movement that can lead to the establishment of democratic global institutions, creating space for global political discourse and decision-making. In both instances cosmopolitanism suggest that all individuals belong to a single community rooted in a shared morality, and therefore calls for inclusive, moral, economic, and political relations between individuals on both a local and international level. One way in which the formation of such a global identity politics, rooted in a shared cognitive worldview, has been used in the struggle against the "race to the bottom" is through what Keck and Sikkink (1998) call "transnational advocacy networks" (TANs). These TANs link Third World activists with more empowered political actors and groups in the First World who have more leverage in influencing decisions regarding global economic dynamics, and which can operate outside the control of state and local authorities.

NIKE CORPORATION AND ALLEGATIONS
OF SWEATSHOP LABOR

Until recently, where and under what conditions consumer goods were made had been obscured from mainstream consciousness. The initiating incident that sparked awareness occurred in 1996 when talk-show hostess Kathie

Lee Gifford was caught in a controversy after it was revealed that some of the clothing line sold under her name at Wal-Mart was made under substandard and illegal working conditions in Honduras (Harris and McKay 1996). Reacting to her admission that most celebrities who endorse goods have no knowledge of where or how they are produced, activists increased pressure not only on her and Wal-Mart, but also on other celebrities and the MNCs they represent to help improve conditions at the factories where the products are made.

Nike Corporation, the world's leading supplier of athletic shoes and apparel, in particular became a primary target of condemnation. This was in part due to its visibility through aggressive marketing and advertising campaigns that made its swoosh logo ubiquitous, as well as its multi-million dollar contracts with superstar endorsers such as Michael Jordan, Charles Barkley, Bo Jackson, and Tiger Woods. The success of Nike demonstrates that, as proposed by several theorists of postmodernism, images are now central to social and economic activities and consumption has become as much a social and cultural process as an economic one. Nike shoes are sold mainly for their symbolic value—estimates are that only 15% of all athletic footwear is sold for athletic purposes (SGMA 1999).

Nike was founded in 1964 by CEO Phil Knight and grew tremendously, turning huge profits quickly. Its revenues soared from $5 million in 1975 to $750 million in 1980 to $4 billion in 1993, and reached $9 billion in 1996 (Nike Annual Report 1996). By the early 1990s it had become recognized as the "most powerful force in sports." In 1993 its revenues were larger than the *combined* revenues of Major League Baseball, the National Basketball Association, and the National Football League (Katz 1994: 13).

The corporation demonstrates consumer capitalism par excellence. The focus has always been on developing a well-defined identity and one which expresses a sense of physical and emotional empowerment through health and fitness, transmitting these cultural values and images to its product (Korzeniewicz 1992). Additionally, its slogans and images representative of individual achievement, hedonism, diversity, authenticity, irreverence, empowerment, narcissism, and the pursuit of pleasure have served as the backbone of Nike advertising (Carty 2005). Nike's television and print advertising campaigns have been hailed as some of the most successful, creative, and inspirational. In 1995 it was named marketer of the year by *Advertising Age*, its name ranking among the world's top ten brands (Jensen 1996). Its longest running and most successful campaign, "Just Do It," was chosen by *Advertising Age* as one of the top five ad slogans of the twentieth century. Recognizing the importance of marketing and advertising, and its relationship to consumer capitalism, CEO Knight stated: "You don't sell a shoe by talking about how well it's stitched. . . . The seismic sociological shift by which American kids of the last one quarter of the twentieth century have been turned into ritualistically brand-conscious consumers is as much due to television as a change created by Nike and other companies with similar bottom-line desires" (Katz 1994: 264).

Nike also gained exposure by moving beyond individual contracts with athletes and solidifying endorsement deals with entire teams and universities. One of the most lucrative was a $7 million deal with the University of Michigan football team (Featherstone 2002). By 1994 twenty-three of the top twenty-five college teams were outfitted by Nike and in 1996 it had two-hundred and fifty colleges under contract, making it the number one licenser in college sports apparel (Baum 1996).

The Anti-Nike Campaign

Unlike many other U.S.-based corporations, Nike did not *relocate* its manufacturing base to developing countries. It imported shoes from Asia form its inception and the emphasis has always been on distribution, design, and marketing. By 1999 it had contracting arrangements with over seven-hundred factories, most located in Indonesia, China, and Vietnam (Klein 2000). Over 80% of its workforce is female, most of whom are under the age of twenty-five (pressforchange.org).

In the mid-1990s scholars, labor rights activists, and journalists began citing numerous systematic violations of worker rights in Nike factories. These included health and safety deficiencies, discrimination against trade unions, forced overtime, paying below the local minimum wage, corporal and verbal abuse, and the use of hire-and-fire practices to avoid paying fringe benefits, and on-site living arrangements that were both inadequate and dangerous. News reports of these working conditions appeared regularly in the popular press. In 1996 *Life Magazine* ran a front cover story that documented children in Pakistan as young as six stitching and sewing Nike soccer balls (Rao 1997). CBS ran an episode on its program *Street Stories* in 1993 that lambasted Nike for the working conditions in its sub-contracted factories. Later, the network's program *48 Hours* ran a segment on factories in Vietnam where journalists discovered that Nike was paying below minimum wage wages, workers were subject to compulsory over-time, and there were several instances of physical and verbal abuse (Dobnik 1997). During the 1998 Olympics ESPN aired an *Outside the Lines* episode which featured interviews and tours that documented sweatshop abuse allegations in Nike factories in Vietnam.

Political cartoons lampooned the accusations against Nike for using child labor to stitch soccer balls in Cambodia and Pakistan, and these accusations were also exposed in a 2000 BBC documentary (Rao 1997). Between May and October of 1997 Garry Trudeau's *Doonesbury* comic strip featured a series on Nike, making humorous critique of its overseas controversies, its self-commissioned monitoring system, the use of hand-picked interpreters to translate worker grievances, the outrageous salaries of Nike endorsers, the omnipresence of the Nike swoosh logo on teams and individual endorsers such as Tiger Woods, and the growing protest movement against Nike facilitated through the Protest Nike site on the Internet.

Much of the coverage in the mainstream media further acknowledged that the biggest factor in the cost of Nike shoes and apparel was money spent on advertising and endorsement sponsorships. At this time Nike was spending $650 million on marketing a year (not including the hundreds of millions paid to its endorsers)—ten times what it would cost the company to double wages of all Indonesian workers (Moberg 1997). The $25 million Nike was paying to Michael Jordan alone in 1994 was the same the company spent in Indonesia for the labor to make nineteen million pairs of Nike shoes that same year, whereas 2% of Nike's marketing budget could have increased the salary of all 25,000 workers from $1.60 to $3 a day, thus putting them above the poverty line (pressforchange.org).

Describing Nikes involvement in the "race to the bottom" on ABC's *Nightline* Ted Koppel summarized: "manufactures set out find the lowest paid workers wherever in the world they may be. And if those happen to be children in Senegal, or Indonesia, Pakistan, or Guatemala, it is difficult to remember when we are mesmerized by a television campaign with Jordan soaring to the basket in his Nikes" (*Nightline* 1996). This again supports claims made by theorists of postmodernism who view much of social and cultural life as based on simulations and, according to Baudrillard specifically, surface oftentimes trumps depth.

A series of critical books focusing on Nike were also published at this time. Naomi Klein's *No Logo* (2000) and filmmaker Michael Moore's *Downsize This* (1996), both best sellers on the *New York Times* best seller list, singled out Nike as one of the top violators of worker rights. *Reclaiming America* by Randy Shaw (1999) and *No Sweat* by Andrew Ross (1997) also addressed Nike's involvement with sweatshops and lack of corporate social responsibility. In Moore's movie, *The Big One* (2002), he interviewed Phil Knight who admitted that he had never been to Indonesia (where the bulk of Nike shoes and apparel were being produced), and stated that he felt it was acceptable for fourteen-year-old girls to be assembling Nike merchandise. The film, as well as the books, also pointed out the hypocrisy regarding Nike advertising messages of empowerment and rebellion as opposed to the working conditions in its factories. The phrase "Just Do It" contained a very different meaning for assembly line workers than it did for First World consumers.

Major national newspapers such as *The New York Times, The Los Angeles Times, The Washington Post, The San Francisco Examiner,* and *The Wall Street Journal* carried op-ed pieces as well as general coverage of the allegations against Nike throughout the 1990s. In 1997 *The New York Times* reported in a front-page story that Ernst & Young accounting firm, after monitoring conditions at plants owned by Nike contractors in Vietnam, found them to be "dismal" (Drier and Appelbaum 2003).

Nike also received negative attention via electronic forms of media. For example, in 2001 MIT graduate student Jonah Peretti, in an e-mail to

Nike, requested the word "sweatshop" be stitched onto his shoes (Peretti 2001). Nike had begun offering this service on its website so that consumers could personalize their footwear. In its response the company declared that for a number of "technical" reasons (such as the word sweatshop being slang), it could not accommodate his request. Peretti replied by providing Nike with the definition of sweatshop that he referenced from Webster's dictionary. After several exchanges Nike admitted that the reason for rejecting the request was that the company reserved the right to reject anything "we consider inappropriate or simply do not want to place on our products." The final response from Peretti was, "Could you send a color snapshot of the ten-year old Vietnamese girl who makes my shoes?" (Peretti 2001).

Peretti e-mailed the series of electronic correspondence to twelve friends and within a period of a few weeks it reached millions of people. At the height of circulation Peretti was receiving five-hundred messages a day from all six continents. His exchange is an example of how ordinary citizens can use forms of micro-media to reach others in the new networked economy with limited or no cost. At first, articles about the correspondence appeared in progressive and technology-oriented publications such as Salon.com, *The Village Voice*, and *In These Times*. This quickly filtered up from the micro-media to the mass media. For example, *Time Magazine*, *The Los Angeles Times*, *The Wall Street Journal*, *Business Week*, and NBC's *Today Show* all covered the story.

As the news reports about the corporation continued and citizens began to look behind the sleek advertising messages to examine its overseas business practices, the symbolic nature of the brand name became increasingly endangered. By the mid 1990s even "charity" in the form of donations by Nike was denied by local governments and school systems. For example, its donation of $500,000 to support the school district in Portland was declined as well as its proposal to build a $50,000 gym floor for a community center in Ottawa (Bulman 1996; Campaign of Labor Rights 1998). In New York City a coalition of young people organized a campaign asking consumers to donate their old Nike shoes to the Bronx community center, where they would be collected and returned to the NIKETOWN on Fifth Avenue in downtown Manhattan (Dwyer 1996). The campaign criticized Nike for failing to pay workers a living wage while charging urban teenagers up to $180 for the shoes (Moberg 1997).

What ultimately developed was an umbrella Working Group on Nike made up of an amalgamation of smaller groups and campaigns (Shaw 1999). This included the Interfaith Center of Corporate Responsibility, the National Labor Committee, Campaign for Labor Rights, the United Methodist Church Pension Fund, the National Organization of Women, Amnesty International's group 48 (Portland), Justice, Do it Nike!, local chapters of Jobs with Justice, Peaceworks, Press for Change, Global Exchange, East Timor Action Network and several other NGOs. A common theme emerged among the different segments of the movement: to shame the corporation and demand global corporate social responsibility.

Many of these NGOs coordinated efforts with students at the high school and college level, including Global Exchange (GE) and Campaign for Labor Rights (CLR), and it was the Internet that facilitated the mobilization. Press for Change mailed press kits to campus newspapers at colleges, universities, as well as to high school social studies teachers with news clippings and guidelines for setting up meetings with retailers (pressforchange.org). GE and Press for Change jointly organized a five-city speaking tour that hosted Chi Abad, a fired Nike worker who attempted to form a union at a Nike-producing factory in Saipan.

GE also put out frequent "Action Alerts" on its website with information of where and when protest activities would take place and provided a list of alternative brands that sell footwear and apparel that had more responsible business practices. The site also offered a Campaign starter kit, which consisted of a petition letter to Nike CEO Phil Knight, a city anti-sweatshop resolution, a sample student government resolution, a sample letter to the editor, and recent accomplishments of activist strategies. It encouraged students to start a Nike campaign on college campuses, assisted in planning demonstrations at sports events, organized petition drives, and encouraged Nike Teach-ins to increase awareness in local communities.

CLR also maintained a very thorough website throughout the campaign that offered online action packets regarding international forms of mobilization. The packets included informative fact sheets, sample press releases, a flier master for promoting events, and Nike Mobilization reports from local communities regarding international mobilizations. Internet postings by CLR on its "Boycott Nike" site organized informational leafleting and provided the address and number of Nike headquarters, a petition, and press and media reports on working conditions.

The Internet also assisted in the *global* mobilization against Nike. Consumer awareness campaigns emerged in Holland, Germany, Canada, the United Kingdom, France, Italy, and Australia. On October 18th of 1997 CLR organized a global protest outside of Nike retailers which was organized electronically—twelve countries and over eighty-four communities and campuses participated (Jenkins 1998). In London, Sweatshop Madness, the Socialist Alliance, and NO SWEAT targeted soccer team sponsorships in the United Kingdom—Nike's endorsement of Manchester United at the time was the biggest sponsorship in soccer history (Shaw 1999). Media coverage of the October 18th event included an AP story, a front page story in *The New York Times* sports section, and a full story in *USA Today*.

Nike's Response and the Emergence of USAS

Nike's initial response to the allegations was to deny them and then insist that the abuses were not the company's responsibility but that of the subcontractors (Shaw 1999). Only after numerous groups mobilized (and called for a nationwide boycott of Nike products), and the company's bottom line was affected by its damaged image, would it finally accept responsibility. In 1998 it implemented a code of conduct that its subcontractors would be subject to. Before the National Press Club, Knight acknowledged the harm that was being done not only to its profits but also to its image and described his company's product as, "synonymous with slave wages, forced overtime, and arbitrary abuse" (Canizares 2001). Among a number of other provisions the code included new health and safety standards, the minimum age was raised to eighteen for full-time employees and sixteen for part-time ones, and the local minimum wage was guaranteed.

However, the code quickly drew criticism from challengers who claimed that the standards were inadequate, there was lack of enforcement, and the self-monitoring system was unacceptable. Three years after the code was implemented GE reported that only one nonprofit organization had been allowed to audit a single Nike factory, wages were still too low for workers to survive on without working overtime, factories were still employing workers under the age of sixteen, many subcontractors were demanding seventy-hour workweeks, and the right to organize was not being recognized (Canizares 2001). For anti-sweatshop activists the code represented nothing more than a PR move in an attempt by Nike to save its image and stop the consequent slump in sales and stock price (Shaw 1999).

One of the strongest criticisms came from USAS which was established in 1998 due to the outreach by the labor movement and NGOs that were already involved in the anti-Nike campaign. Beginning in 1995 United Needle Trades and Industrial Textile Employees (UNITE) and the American Federation of Labor and Congress of International Organizations (AFL-CIO) started training students in labor history and organizational tactics across the United States through summer internships. Through this Union Summer Program students worked as union staffers and representatives on labor campaigns (Shaw 1999). Many returned to school in the fall and organized on their campuses to challenge the collegiate licensing industry (the mediator between manufactures and universities) and pressure them to adopt a code of conduct that all licensees would have to adhere to. Hundreds of universities responded by implementing a code that outlawed the use of sweatshops in their licensing programs (Featherstsone 2002). However, students complained that the code lacked an independent monitoring structure, did not include disclosure of production sites, and there was no mention of support for workers' rights to form independent unions.

They began to pressure university administrators to disregard the licensing code and adopt stronger school codes. Students negotiated these codes with school administrators and practiced various forms of civil disobedience when universities and colleges showed reluctance. Because Nike was the number one licenser and its code was viewed as unacceptable, the movement also pressured administrators to end contracts with Nike specifically.

The first widely publicized mobilization was organized at the University of California at Irvine. In 1996 its student government passed an anti-Global Sweatshop Resolution, and students, professors, and alumni picketed outside of the nearby NIKETOWN (Thao 1996). They also organized a letter-writing campaign to Phil Knight and the U.S. Congress, calling for bilateral trade talks to pressure Congress to get Vietnam to enforce labor laws in all new trade agreements, and petitioned the university administration to remove all Nike products from the campus bookstore (Tsang 1996). Also in 1996 pro-labor groups at the University of Maryland and the University of North Carolina—Chapel Hill held protests and rallies outside of home football games to pressure administrators to hold Nike accountable for its overseas working conditions (Briggs 1996).

Duke University was the first school to establish its own code of conduct that guaranteed the freedom to organize, a requirement for licensees to disclose to the university a complete listing of sites that had any role in the manufacturing process, and independently monitored factories which would encompass all of the university's licenses (Drier and Appelbaum 2003). As more and more universities followed Duke's lead, and students began communicating and mobilizing across campuses at the national level to institute a universal school code, in 1998 USAS was formally established.

Once again the Internet proved to be a critical resource. On the USAS website, activists were able to download USAS organizing manuals from USAS, CLR, and UNITE. These organizing tools included information on how to organize a campus campaign, the USAS model codes of conduct, protest chants, sample fliers, fashion show scripts, petitions, plans for civil disobedience, educational anti-sweatshop workshops, updated FLA critiques, and an entire list of school contact information including e-mail addresses of college presidents. Students were able request a copy of the contract universities had with Nike, to share advice on how to pressure regents and athletic directors to suspend licensing contracts until Nike improved labor practices, and how to adopt a code of conduct that school licensees and manufacturers must abide by. Finally, it provided links to nearly seventy other sites including activist groups against both sweatshops and consumerism.

The AIP, FLA, and WRC

Meanwhile, reacting to growing citizen discontent about labor abuses overseas, in 1996 the Clinton administration (in conjunction with a coalition of apparel companies, unions, and human rights groups) created a unified code of conduct for the overall garment industry through the AIP (Apparel Industry Partnership) and a monitoring body that would enforce it, the FLA (Fair Labor Association). This was founded in 1999 and is made up of representatives of six companies, six NGOs, and three universities. The FLA soon began petitioning universities to join as members (for a fee) under the assumption that this would appease students and allow administrators to avoid any further conflict (Greenhouse 1999). However, like the previous codes, students soon realized that there were some serious flaws in the standards and monitoring system. For example, the provisions allowed companies to choose their own monitors, select which of their contract shops would be monitored, and to keep the results to themselves (Bacon 2001). Thus companies could certify by their own accord that their products were "sweat free."

Given the shortcomings and what many perceived as a PR whitewash due to the significant corporate presence and voluntary self-monitoring of the FLA, labor, human rights, religious groups, and students formed a rival entity, the Workers Rights Consortium (WRC). The WRC is made up only of university representatives and NGOs (no corporate presence), demands full disclosure of all licensees' factory sites, a living (rather than the minimum) wage, and independent monitoring based on *verifying* worker complaints rather than *certifying* specific factories or companies (Featherstone 2002).

Students view the WRC as a more genuine, democratic, and transparent approach to combating sweatshops because control is shared equally by universities, USAS, and an advisory council made up of human rights groups, labor unions, and academics. Many universities, however, were reluctant to jeopardize licensing deals that would result from joining the WRC. For example, as the movement gained momentum and students successfully pressured a number of universities to drop out of the FLA and become a member of the WRC Nike began to retaliate. It cancelled exclusive and multi-million dollar contracts with Brown University, Texas University, the University of Michigan, and the University of Oregon (Phil Knight's alma mater). Knight lashed out at the University of Oregon after reneging on a $30 million donation to help build a new basketball arena for "meddling in the world economy where I make my living" (Backman and Hunsberger 2008).

Also, Nike began using the Internet to disrupt student disruptions at NIKETOWNs through Internet surveillance. Its personnel monitored the websites of activist groups and heightened security when aware of upcoming protests. When ten college activists undertook a cross-country "Truth Tour" with a fired Dominican garment worker from New York to Nike headquarters in Beavertown, Oregon, to protest at various NIKETOWNs, they were confronted with local police that were already in place to sabotage their planned rallies. The activists had broadcast a daily Webcast of their adventure, modeled after MTV's "Road Rules" (Featherstone 2002). Personnel also videotaped the first stop in New York City which broke out into a melee in the store as protesters dropped banners, leafleted, and chanted anti-Nike slogans. They relayed the tape, along with bios of the activists (which they downloaded from the Truth Tour website) to police all along the route, who were therefore able to greet the students by name as they attempted to enter the store and let them know they were not welcome (Featherstone 2002).

In response to the temerity of universities to join the WRC students once again engaged in various forms of civil disobedience. They created shanty towns and mock sewing assembly lines, occupied administration buildings, held sit-ins, chained themselves together at various strategic locations on campuses, held protests and rallies, went on hunger strikes, attended nude parties, undertook nude cycling, duct taped their mouths shut symbolizing administrators' refusal to discuss the issue with them, and held mock fashion shows and "smash the swoosh" piñata parties (Featherstone 2002). They also initiated global witnessing campaigns and delegations, traveling to Mexico, Nicaragua, and Honduras to meet with labor activist and garment industry workers to develop international networks. By the fall of 2001 ninety institutions had signed up with the WRC (the FLA had one-hundred and fifty-six). As of now, the WRC has one-hundred and seventy-five members as opposed to the FLA's two-hundred (usas@yahoogroups.com).

The First Test of the WRC: The Kukdong Factory

By the early 2000s student mobilizing efforts shifted from one of demanding corporate social responsibility to one of empowering workers' efforts to unionize. In January of 2001 9,800 workers went on strike at the Korean-owned Kukdong factory located in Puebla, Mexico, in reaction to a host of substandard conditions including the use of child labor, failure to pay the minimum wage, and the firing of union leaders who attempted to form an independent union (Bacon 2001). Workers were also forced to sign with the government-managed (corporatist) union in order to be employed. Mexico had one of the oldest one-party governments in the world and has historically combined repressive production sites with political exclusion to secure a safe environment for foreign investment (Bandy and Mendez 2003).

After a three-day strike a police crackdown ensued and state police attacked the workers; fifteen were hospitalized and the five organizers were fired. When the strike ended and workers returned, they faced intimidation, and in some cases refusal to be reemployed (Schrader 2002). Representatives of USAS and the WRC, in conjunction with WRC's independent monitoring agency called Verite, went to the Kukdong factory and verified the workers' complaints (Campaign for Labor Rights 2002). Nike was the largest manufacturer doing business with Kukdong, producing sweatshirts for many big-name universities. Students pressured administrators to threaten Nike with termination of contracts if it did not help to rectify the situation. They also contacted the Mexico City office of the AFL-CIO, which helped Kukdong workers publicize their case on U.S. and Canadian campuses (Bacon 2001).

Global support was also provided for the workers through the Support Centre (CAT) in Mexico, students at the Autonomous University of Puebla, the AFL-CIO, Campaign for Labor Rights, the U.S. Labor Education in the Americas Project (US/LEAP), Sweatshop Watch, the European Clean

Clothes Campaign, Global Exchange, the Maquila Solidarity Network, and the Korean House of International Solidarity. These NGOs provided an overarching forum for the exchange of information and communication among activists that helped expedite the campaign and enhance coalition building. Nike received letters from over six thousand people for seventeen countries. The company eventually took responsibility and declared it would not abandon production orders at Kukdong but preferred the situation be rectified between management and workers through legal proceedings. It devised a plan outlining the corrective actions a timetable for Kukdong to comply with the stipulations (Maquila Solidarity Network 2001). Charges were dropped against two of the five leaders of the strike and workers gained legal recognition of an independent union—the first in any of the free trade zones in Mexico—and received a wage increase of 10% which was 40% more pay that they made under the old contract (Kidd 2001).

The mobilization to sustain the workers' campaign was a multi-level, multi-task strategy targeting the local, national, and international level that embraced both contentious and institutional politics. At the local level the workers staged a walkout to disrupt the accumulation of capital at the level of production and students pressured university administrators at the level of consumption. At the national level, in solidarity with the workers, activists lobbied the Labor Secretary in Mexico and the Mexican Cabinet Secretary and students mobilized through USAS. And globally, they pressured the Global Director for Labor Practices at Nike, Kukdong International (Mexico), and Kukdong Corporation Korea (Korea) to resolve the dispute. International solidarity at the grassroots level unequivocally played a significant role in the success.

What made this cross national, synerginistic mobilization possible was the Internet. Daily updates of the events in Puebla were posted on the USAS listserve and USAS website consisting of press releases, pictures, and video documentation (Kidd 2001). USAS also organized a Kukdong listserve, which allowed activists to respond immediately to changing conditions and to lend support in real time. Subscribers to the various listserves were given information on how to contact Nike and Kukdong directly. They were prompted to demand that management at the factory comply with Mexican labor laws, Nike's code of conduct, the respective universities' codes of conduct, and the international agreement regarding the rights of freedom to organize. E-mail addresses were made available for letters of solidarity to workers, and for contacting the Labor Secretary in Mexico, the Global Director for Labor Practices at Nike, the Senior Labor Practices Manager at Nike, Kukdong International (Mexico), Kukdong Corporation Korea (Korea), and the Mexican Cabinet Secretary. The web resistance emulates what Arquilla and Ronfeldt refer to as an NGO swarm: "One that has no central leadership or structure, is decentralized, impossible to eliminate. And can sting a victim to death" (Arquilla and Ronfeldt 1999).

The Internet further assisted the struggle through Nike's own website. Under pressure from students and administrators at some of the largest colleges and universities, Nike conceded to publish on its site the location of factories producing for the particular schools that had requested this information (the first company ever to do so in the entire garment industry). After checking the site many students discovered that Kukdong was producing sweatshirts for several of the universities most heavily involved with the USAS campaign. This facilitated a quick response among students in the struggle and provided them with leverage to pressure university administrators to cancel or suspend their contracts with Nike and/or to acknowledge that the FLA was not an adequate monitoring devise, as Kukdong was a "certified" factory according to Nike's self-monitoring.

LINKING PRODUCTION AND CONSUMPTION: MICRO-MEDIA AND CULTURE JAMMERS

Whereas the anti-sweatshop movement seeks to reform the system from within to create a more humane form of corporate capitalism, other activists argue that a truly counter-hegemonic movement must not only embrace changing institutional arrangements, but also proactively advocate a different value system. This is one which calls for a transformation in the way citizens think about consumerism and the social and cultural implications and oppose what Sklair (1998) refers to as the "cultural ideology of consumption." He argues that this is the ideology which "generates and maintains global capitalism and fosters values and attitudes that create and sustain the need for consumer goods, commercializing and commodifying all ideas and the material products in which they adhere" (94). An authentic anti-capitalism global system movement is one that challenges MNCs in the economic sphere, international bureaucrats and local affiliates in the political sphere, and promotes ideologies opposed to capitalist consumerism. The starting point is for individuals and activists to reject marketing, reclaim the communication industries, and challenge the capitalist principle of the unlimited accumulation of private profit.

The anti-consumption movement therefore represents a more radical rethinking of the assumptions that drive the capitalist global system and is more aligned with cultural strands of NSM theory and framing. It attempts to create a greater awareness of why the present conditions exist, how they got to be this way, whose purposes they serve, and how the manufacturing of consent works through the manipulation of symbols. The global movement, Culture Jammers, is one of the leading advocates this philosophy. It is aimed at exposing questionable political assumptions behind commercial culture— logos, fashion statements, and product image—and for transparency about a product or company in order to convert easily identifiable images into larger questions about such matters as global social responsibility (Lasn 1999).

Culture Jamming is mainly a symbolic form of protest that combats what activists view as the undemocratic principles of corporate domination and the principles of the market (McDonald 2002). Such symbolic forms of contentious politics include targeting symbols that represent consumer goods and transform them into in an alternative context. It calls for a shift in perspective on consumer capitalism and economic globalization as well a shift in emotional investment in attitude toward consumption.

Kalle Lasn, one of the leaders of Culture Jammers, describes jamming as "semiological guerilla warfare" and a self-proclaimed "The People Versus the Corporate Cool Machine" (Lasn 1999: xvi). Focusing on both production and consumption, jammers disseminate information regarding business practices of particular MNCs and their products, and then use this information to "uncool" the product and/or brand. Their magazine, *Adbuster*, lampoons and parodies ads by distributing "uncommercials" that subvert advertising messages. The Nike uncommercial below parodies a series of Nike print ads that targeted the women's market by emphasizing

Figure 2.1   Courtesy Adbusters Media foundation.

liberation, independence, and empowerment. It plays on the fact that most workers assembling Nike products are female, young, and exploited.

Jammers mobilize in both cyberspace and in the material world. Posters that they produce highlighting the undemocratic nature of the corporate-controlled economic, cultural, and social space can be downloaded from their website and hung in local communities. The Independence Day Flag Jam poster (a corporate U.S. flag) was hung on a six-hundred square foot Manhattan billboard and throughout major urban centers on July 4, 2001. It was designed with the logos of fifty of the leading MNCs rather than stars for the fifty states, and the Nike swoosh is at the center of the configuration.

NIKETOWNs and Nike billboards have been subject to urban graffiti steadily in the United States, Canada, Australia, Sweden, and the United Kingdom. A billboard advertisement for Nike soccer boots in Stockholm was jammed twice. Graffiti artists added the tagline "Just Don't Do It" the first time, and "bojkott" (boycott) the second time after it was restored to its original state. These types of contentious politics are what Best and Kellner refer to as micro-politics and problematize Baudrillard's claims that consumer goods, because they are primarily sold as symbols, form their own kind of reality. As the Jammers show, by deconstructing and targeting forces of decentered power, new areas of social and personal areas can open up for rationalist critique and resistance. They furthermore illustrate that there *is* room for human agency as simulations can be exposed once deconstructed and power is not necessarily abstract.

THEORETICAL ASSESSMENT OF THE STRUGGLE

Overall, the anti-Nike campaign can be viewed as relatively successful. The corporation eventually admitted responsibility for overseas working conditions, disclosed factory locations, and acquiesced to certain demands made by USAS and the WRC (perhaps most importantly to recognize the right to freedom of association). Although international and Mexico's own labor laws mandate workers' legal right to organize, it took disruptive action by workers, mobilizing in solidarity with other activists, to enforce it at Kukdong. Illustrating the impact that the anti-Nike campaign had, Maria Eitel, VP of corporate responsibility for Nike, declared, "I don't think Nike would have made the kind of progress it has made if we hadn't been attacked" (Cave 2002).

There were several variables that enabled the mobilization. These included taking advantage of existing political opportunities, choosing successful tactics to increase awareness and shame the company, having a clearly defined set of goals, and having access to internal and external resources. After years of struggle the target of collective action was forced to recognize the challengers as legitimate representatives of a constituency, thereby altering the relationship between the activists/workers and Nike. Participants in the movement were also successful in tapping into existing values and public opinion regarding the use of sweatshop labor and consumer preferences as represented in the PIPA poll. Additionally, the movement had all four central components a successful social movement as outlined by Tilly (1973): there was a sense of worthiness, unity, numbers, and commitment.

It is the interconnected dimension of social movement theories that best explain the success, each of which illuminates a different aspect of the dynamics of the mobilization. Political process directs our attention to the political context within which collective behavior is shaped, including which claims will be pursued, alliances formed, and strategies and tactics chosen (Amenta and Caren 2004; Kresi 2004; McAdam 1982; Tilly 1973). In the case of Kukdong workers had an insurgent consciousness and some (relatively minimal) resources, but political opportunities were for the most part closed due to government repression. Although in 2000 the seventy-one year rule of the PRI (Institutional Revolutionary Party) was voted out of power, because of the novelty of the transition the government was still not as receptive or vulnerable to disruptive tactics that may have been the case in a well-established democracy. This supports Tarrow's (1996) suggestion of the necessity of open political systems for successful social movement outcomes.

On the other hand, with the end of the consolidation of power activists were able to take advantage of what slight opening there was to petition members of the Mexican government to adhere to national and international law. This was complimented by activists outside of Mexico doing the same. What gave workers the most leverage was pressure on the government from outside the country directly and indirectly (lobbying Nike, retailers, universities, and South Korean subcontractors to take action). Also, logistically, the proximity of the border between Mexico and the United States offered further opportunities for local resistance because it made international support feasible. This combination of closed domestic POS and an open international POS emulates what Keck and Sikkink (1998) refer to as the "boomerang effect."

The international networking among activists as the mobilization developed is also represented of what Keck and Sikkink (1998) call TANs (transnational action networks) alliances through which more empowered citizens in the First World can work in solidarity to help empower those in the Global South by focusing their efforts not only on the struggles of workers in the Third World, but also on those who set the policies in the First World. Speaking at the University of Michigan, Marcel Peepar (a seamstress at the Kukdong factory) stated, "Without the dialogue at the University of Michigan it would have been impossible to win the struggle. This is one of the reasons we continued to struggle . . . because we knew we had your support" (Schrader 2002, p. D 20).

Meyer and Minkoff (2004) and McAdam (1996) clarify the distinctive role of open or closed informal structures of power relations and of specific constituencies within the political process paradigm. One of the reasons for the strong sense of solidarity between U.S. and Mexican labor groups, as well as the coalitions that were formed between labor and students in the United States, is that the "race to the bottom" had led to a tremendous loss of manufacturing jobs in the United States, shifting political and economic dynamics within the global system. This resulted in a fortuitous opening for workers and activists to work in solidarity across borders as the common enemy was viewed as a political and economic system that demanded little if any responsibility on behalf of governments, corporations, and subcontractors for working conditions.

The resource mobilization framework focuses on the ability of social movement actors to secure and strategically utilize resources. In addition to key resources such as knowledge, money, time, labor power, and media attention, this theory also recognizes external support as a key variable in that it can expand the movement's base (Gamson 1990; McCarthy and Zald 1977; Oslon 1971), and the organizational forms and practices actors adopt (Ganz 2004; Gamson 1990; Staggenborg 1988; Piven and Cloward 1977). The coming together of transnational networks that included workers, students, NGOs, labor organizations, and faith-based organizations played a central role in each of these three dimensions.

Cultural variables such as framing and collective identity are also recognized as key to the sustainability of social movements (Ryan and Gamson 2006; White 1999; Benford and Hunt 1992; Snow et al. 1988). Snow's (1986) conceptualization of framing (prognosis, diagnosis, and motivational) was evident in the struggle. The prognosis was stated clearly as corporate greed and lack of oversight of working conditions, the diagnosis was the end of sweatshop labor, independent monitoring, and support of workers' struggles for unionization, and the motivating variable was corporate shaming to force Nike to adopt social responsibility for its working condition. Frame bridging, another term introduced by Snow (1986), was also demonstrated as activists articulated concerns that resonated with citizens regarding corporate social responsibility as shown in the PIPA survey.

A sense of collective identity fueled the campaign, and as emphasized by several scholars such as Polletta and Jasper (2001), Snow and McAdam (2000), Japser (1977), and Klandermans (1977). This can be a perceived rather than a direct connection to those suffering from injustice. This is often rooted in a broad sense of ethical or moral concerns. In the anti-Nike campaign, youth groups and students identified with people roughly their age working long hours under horrendous conditions. Women's groups (including the National Organization of Women) identified with female laborers and issues of sexism. Asian groups (and especially student groups on college campuses) identified with Asian workers and were sympathetic to the racist underpinnings of wealthy First World-based MNCs using Third World labor to produce their goods. Labor groups were sympathetic to restrictions on collective bargaining. And finally, human rights and faith-based groups, as well as large investors connected with ethical issues, joined the struggle on the basis of values and compassion. Although the groups were fragmented, their concerns were channeled into a cohesive focus and strategy, making this vast extension of identity politics into a politically strong and effective coalition.

This mobilization can also be understood through the lens of new social movement theory and the ideology of cosmopolitanism because it illustrates that collective identity can be forged through a common sense of values and a shared cognitive world view on both a local and global scale. Many scholars view NSMs as a reaction to the deepening of domination under capitalism and the global nature of many social problems, which leads to a convergence of multi-class and multi-identity based struggles (Giddens 1991; Offe 1985). The mobilization against Nike took on a form of what Evans (2000) refers to as globalized identity politics whereby individuals and groups with similar identities and interests form flexible and pluralistic transnational networks. Jameson's (1984) notion of a "radical politics for now" is also useful in understanding how individuals became aware of their individual and collective sense as citizens under multi-national capitalism on a spatial and social scale. Furthermore, Tomlinson's (2002) concept of "distantiated identity" is also relevant as the various groups involved in the campaign embraced a sense of mutual responsibility and a compassionate perspective through an increased consciousness of the structural arrangements of global capitalism. Workers, labor coalitions, and other activists in the United States and elsewhere recognized that their well-being was inherently tied to workers in developing countries under the mechanics of the "race to the bottom."

Culture Jammers are indicative of the cultural strand of NSM theory in that they acknowledge the decentralized nature of power and undertake symbolic forms of resistance within civil society in a struggle over the process of meaning, relationships, and personal change. Their participation in the movement highlights the proposition of scholars who contend that such symbols challenge forms of domination alongside institutionalized contestation and attempt to defend the public sphere (see Cohen 1985; Touraine 1985; Habermas 1983). They further buttress suggestions in the literature that new social movement activists are addressing new issues, distilling new values, operate in new areas and employ new modes of action through loosely articulated, decentralized, and egalitarian networks (Castells 1997; Gusfield 1994; Mueller 1994).

By rejecting marketing schemes, reclaiming the communication industries, and challenging the capitalist principle of unlimited accumulation the Culture Jammers and the anti-sweatshop movement together offer a way to bridge the macro/micro link. The agenda employed by both movements is to use grassroots organizing and concrete action to locally resist institutions of economic and cultural exploitation. Thus, they represent a way to address both broad features of social life (the capitalist system) and sources of fragmentation (commercialization and commodification as promoted through marketing strategies).

All of these efforts dispute some of the more pessimist claims made by theories of postmodernism regarding political struggle. Even though social relationships may be dislocated under global capitalism, the anti-Nike campaign demonstrates that people can become aware of the structural arrangements in which they live despite the transformation in the character of power and the accompanying cultural shift. This is in part due to the interdependence, consciousness, and interaction that also takes placed under accelerated processes of globalization through technological advances and the development of new ICTs.

Indeed, the electronic media was an indispensable tool for raising awareness of the problem as well as the grassroots networking among the various groups. Nike spokesperson Veda Manager explained, "You make changes because it's the right thing to do. But obviously our actions have clearly been accelerated by the web" (Klein 2000: 393). The Internet and alternative media gave citizens a way to define social problems in ways not depicted by mainstream media. The Internet to be a medium that enhanced the interconnectedness and consciousness of groups and individuals on a global scale, opening up new possibilities for social relations between workers in developing countries and activists in core countries. It facilitated a form of grassroots democracy that offered a new type of civic engagement, allowing citizens to operate outside of state regulation as espoused by several theorists of the Internet (see Carty 2010, 2009; Dutta-Bergman 2006; Jenkins 2006; Langman 2005; Kellner 2004; Nipp 2004; Kahn and Kellner 2003; Van Aelst and Walgrave 2003; Castells 2001; Diani 2000; Kollock and Smith 1999).

This campaign also highlights that as boundaries become more fluid over cyberspace, coalition-forming becomes easier and new forms of networking can turn into permanent campaigns and result in a spillover affect despite weak social ties. This sustains claims of many scholars of new ICTs such as Smith, Costello, and Brecher (2009), Bennett and Iyengar (2008), Jenkins (2006), Langman (2005), and Nipp (2004). In sum, the anti-sweatshop movement shows that through the formation of global networks and utilization of new forms of digital communication, social movement activists are increasingly enabled to think locally and act globally by contesting sources of power where the power holders are located.

3 Contentious Politics, Cyberactivism, and Electoral Reform
The Reemergence of the Peace Movement Post 9–11

The National Security Strategy document, or the "Bush Doctrine," which was installed after the 9-ll attacks on the United States, postulated a vision of the United States as the world's unchallenged superpower. It defended the preemptive use of U.S. military power, refusal of the United States to be bound by any international treaty or organization, the ability to violate international laws and disregard international institutions such as the United Nations (UN) when expedient to do so, and explicitly linked U.S. economic and military policy (Peter 2007). Critics charge that it served to accelerate the process of imperial globalization in the name of providing security to U.S. citizens and its allies under the guise of the "war on terrorism" (Gitlin 2005). The war on terrorism, as spelled out by the Bush administration, is defined as the military, political, and legal actions in response to 9–11 with the objective of countering terrorist threats, preventing terrorist acts, and curbing the influence of terrorist organizations (whitehouse.gov).

Former President Bush consistently referred to the 2003 invasion of Iraq as one of the central fronts in the war on terrorism (Peter 2007). After failing to get approval by the United Nations (UN) for the invasion, the administration's attempt to assemble a "coalition of the willing" became critical to the battle for public opinion to back the war. Shortly before the Iraq war began, the U.S. government announced that nearly forty countries had joined the coalition. However, only four contributed troops—Britain, Poland, Australia, and Denmark—more than 95% of the committed combat troops were American or British (Ripley 2008).

Key countries on the UN Security Council, most notably France and Russia, did not support the coalition from the onset and as the conflict dragged on politicians and citizens in countries that originally supported the invasion began to question the war and dropped out of the coalition. As global networks of individuals pressured their governments to cooperate in a coalition of the *unwilling,* the coalition eventually unraveled and all combat troops are scheduled to leave Iraq by 2011 in what is perceived as a defeat for the United States (Farrell 2008). Consequently, this raises questions regarding the ability of the United States to operate unilaterally in the future, and what factors were responsible for the demise of the coalition. The United States' success as sole superpower in the past depended on a system of alliances with other powers and a division among those who would challenge it (Owens 2006). However, this has been altered on two fronts. First, at the core of the Bush Doctrine is the replacement of international cooperation with a world order based on direct U.S. assertion that it will act alone if necessary. Second, there emerged a collective opposition to the U.S. invasion, even among former allies, as public opinion increasingly turned against participation in the war on terrorism.

This chapter combines different aspects of social movement theory to examine how the coalition of the unwilling emerged and what effect it had on the failure of the United States to sustain support for the Iraq war. Research mobilization, framing analysis, constructionism, and new social movement theories, as well as theories that focus on social movement consequences can explain *how* the contemporary peace movement forged a sense of transnational collective identity and organized to try to influence public opinion and public authorities through contentious politics. Other theories that employ the political process model illustrate that the collapse of the coalition was also due in part to a "revolution at the ballot box." The political process framework draws attention to the importance of working within the formal arena of institutional and electoral politics. Its emphasis on potential shifts in governance discourse, which allow activists to question states' legitimacy and manipulate competition between political elites, helps to clarify *why* and *when* mobilizations emerge.

Thus, I employ a comprehensive analytical framework and argue that neither resource mobilization nor structural theories on their own can sufficiently explain the demise of the coalition and ultimate defeat of the United States' efforts in Iraq. Instead, structural-, meso- and micro-level mobilization efforts were interconnected in complex ways, and must be theorized as such. Finally, the chapter provides an examination of how contemporary social movements are using ICTs (information communication technologies) as mobilizing tools and conduits to alternative forms of media. I specifically focus on how the Internet and non-profit public interest media sites on the Web served as a central means of communicating grievances, sharing and expanding communication across various transnational constituencies, and ultimately increased the interconnectedness and consciousness of groups and individuals on a global scale.

REACTION TO THE WAR ON TERROR: CONTENTIOUS POLITICS

The Bush-initiated war on terrorism, and the March 20, 2003 invasion of Iraq more explicitly, sparked a reemergence of the peace movement on an international scale. Peace activists have historically utilized a wide range of repertoires that include conventional political activity, protest activities, consciousness raising, moral persuasion, civil disobedience, violence, sabotage, and self-immolation (Marullo and Meyer 2004). Immediately following the 9–11 attacks the most popular forms of mobilization were protests and rallies. These two repertoires are effective in that they dramatize the legitimacy, unity, numbers, and commitment of groups supporting the social movement's goals (McAdam et al. 2001; Jasper 1997; Klandermans 1997; Gamson 1992; Tilly 1973). They also help to consolidate activist identities among new recruits and long term members by dramatizing conflict and creating "us-versus-them" identities as they develop an oppositional consciousness.

The first major protests against the declared war on terrorism took place a few weeks after the 9–11 attacks (anticipating an invasion of Afghanistan by the United States in retaliation) in San Francisco and Washington DC, and were sponsored by ANSWER (Act Now to Stop War and End Racism). ANSWER is one of the largest U.S.-based transnational peace organizations. UFPJ (United for Peace and Justice), another leading U.S.-based and transnational peace organization, was established one year later in response to certain frustrations with ANSWER. Whereas initially the two groups held joint events, because of disputes over issues of framing and agenda, the two had a very public split and currently hold separate protests (for a full description of the discrepancies between the two organizations see Coy, Wohrle, and Maney 2005). In terms of leadership, organizational dynamics, and utilization of resources this has been a hindrance to the peace movement within the United States, but international momentum and activism in other countries has helped to sustain the overall mobilization.

The real acceleration of the peace movement took place two years later, beginning a few months before the invasion of Iraq. Globally, between January 3rd and April 12th of 2003 thirty-six million people across the globe took part in almost 3,000 protests against the war in Iraq (Callincos 2005). The power of protest mobilization was most clearly evident on February 15, 2003 when the world experienced the largest international mobilization for peace ever. This was coordinated simultaneously in seventy-five countries with estimates ranging as high as fifteen million people across all six continents (bbc.com 2003).

One of the largest gatherings took place in London, where over two million people protested in Hyde Park alone (Bowley 2004). In Germany 500,000 protested, 300,000 rallied across France, and tens of thousands demonstrated in Melbourne, the largest peace march the city had witnessed since the Vietnam War (cnn.com). The international protest was one of a series of demonstrations organized by UK-based Stop the War coalition (the UK's largest antiwar organization which serves as an umbrella organization that networks with dozens of other peace, labor, Muslim, and other groups) before and after the invasion of Iraq. This international mobilization demonstrated the efficacy of global solidarity through grassroots protest as thousands of independent yet interconnected groups organized to challenge U.S. foreign policy, as well as the role of their own governments in supporting the war. Dr. Robert Muller (the former assistant secretary general of the United Nations) stated: "Now there are two superpowers: the US and the merging voice of the people of the world. All around the world, people are waging peace. It is nothing short of a miracle and it is working—despite what you may see unfolding in the news" (Hoge 2004). Also following the protest, the *New York Times* described the global peace movement as "the world's second superpower," and it was after this global demonstration that governments of nine countries backed out of arrangements to support the U.S. war against terrorism (Packer 2003).

After the February 15ᵗʰ demonstrations other numerous events and coordinated actions took place to capitalize on the momentum of the protest. On the 16ᵗʰ of February an estimated 400,000 protested in Milan and more than 300,000 took the streets in Barcelona in response to the governments' participation in the coalition of the willing (*New York Times* 2003). On that same day more than 6,000 candlelight vigils for peace were held in more than 100 countries (MoveOn.org). Protests against state visits by President Bush also drew thousands to the streets globally. In November of 2003, 200,000 people protested in Trafalgar Square when President Bush made a state visit to the United Kingdom (*Agence French Press* 2004). When he visited Ireland in 2005, 50,000 citizens protested the use of Shannon Airport as a stopover point for U.S. troops bound for Iraq. When Bush left Shannon for Turkey and then later traveled to Canada he encountered similar scenes of hostility. Some of the most popular signs at protests that questioned the motive for the invasion and displayed resentment toward Bush included slogans such as, "Drop Bush Not Bombs," and "Regime Change Begins at Home" (*Agence French Press* 2004). Ultimately, the target of these protests was the Bush Doctrine and in particular the concept of preemptive war.

Global witnessing was another key strategy that the peace movement utilized. This tactic allows for a pedagogical style that increases awareness about the global context of social problems and helps to create solidarity across borders through public civic education. For example, Fernando Suarez del Solar, who lost his son in the Iraqi war, has been one of the most prominent speakers critiquing the war. He travels internationally with San Francisco-based NGO Global Exchange and several other military families to expose what he feels to be the many lies surrounding the war effort (GlobalExchange.org). Robert Sarra, a veteran of the Iraq war, also became an anti-war activist despite his perception of protesters as hippies who, in his eyes during the Vietnam War protest movement, had "no right to protest and just hated the military" (Chaudry 2004). He is now the co-founder of Iraq Veterans Against the War and canvasses throughout the United States to raise awareness of the realities of the war.

Sarra's comments represent the importance of framing grievances in general terms that appeal to an overall sense of justice, and how increasing awareness of injustice based on first-hand experience can solidify opposition across party lines. He states, "What I've been doing, though, is to stay non-partisan. I've been doing that because people have got to remember that this isn't something political. There are both Democrats and Republicans with kids over there fighting . . . for the guys over there, politics isn't a factor to them. It's about fighting for that guy next to you and getting home in one piece and getting back to your family" (Chaudry 2004). This type of global witnessing from soldiers returning from war helps to humanize the conflict and gives legitimacy to the protesters on the basis of the veterans' personal and firsthand experience in Iraq.

Cyberactivism

Much of the organization driving contentious politics took place in cyberspace. For example, web-based anti-war network WHY WAR delivered news, analysis, strategy, and progressive insight about the war on terrorism. Two key concepts it promotes on its website are "radical empathy" and "swarming." Radical empathy immerses the individual in the struggle of another in order to bridge the gap between "us" and "them" by sharing authentic life-experiences that document different aspects of the global peace movement. The goal is to increase solidarity through a shared sense of morality and consciousness of human rights (WhyWar.org). Swarming involves the tactic of the seemingly spontaneous appearance of anti-war crowds engaging in civil disobedience. This represents a fundamental shift in the mechanics of protests because mobilization can emerge from "free-wheeling amorphous groups rather than top-down hierarchical ones" (Lee 2003).

The fusion of network communications and social networks as facilitated by the Web has also led to the emergence of so-called "smart mobs" headed by organizers who strategize like virtual field commanders (Lee 2003). This strategy was evident on the ground when activists disrupted the 2004 Republican National Convention in New York City, where many gathered to protest the war on terrorism and the invasion of Iraq. Groups such as Counter Convention and Radical Reference acted as resource services providing protest tools and logistical aid to the demonstrators (Scahill 2004). Also, independent journalists and wired activists mobilized by using cell phone text messaging technology to coordinate a campaign of direct action and comprehensive news reporting, sending out action alerts, warnings, and news and announcements directly from the New York Independent Media Center (IMC). The IMC is a network of collectively run grassroots media outlets fuelled by independent journalism that operates in real time and outside of corporate media control.

Some of the most effective grassroots organizing in the peace movement developed exclusively online. For example, Peaceful Tomorrows, founded by family members of 9–11 victims to promote effective, nonviolent solutions to terrorism and to "acknowledge the common experience of all people similarly affected by violence world-wide," initiated their website right after the 9–11 attacks (peacefultommorows.org). On their website they advocate dialogue, education, and consciousness-raising regarding U.S. foreign policy and advocate multilateral approaches to uphold principles of international law. Two other prominent online anti-war organizations, MoveOn.org and Win Without War.org, were also born in cyberspace. Win Without War serves as an online umbrella organization that provides links to dozens of other related pro-peace coalitions, and MoveOn works on a host of progressive issues including the peace movement.

In February 2003 the two social movement organizations held one of the most prominent acts of online civil disobedience—a virtual march to protest the imminent invasion of Iraq. On February 26th 200,000 individuals signed a petition circulated through their e-mail base and made more than 400,000 phone calls and sent 100,000 faxes to each Senator that read: DON'T ATTACK IRAQ! (winwithoutwar.org). Every Senator also received a stream of e-mails that clogged up virtual mailboxes in Washington (Harris 2003). Members of the two groups also petitioned their congressional representatives in every state to investigate the government's controversial claims about the invasion of Iraq and to continue with the inspections for weapons of mass destruction, in addition to organizing thousands of candlelight vigils around the world (Kuttner 2003).

Combining new ICTs with conventional forms of media, right after the 9–11 attacks, MoveOn's website began distributing petitions, e-mail action alerts, letter-to-the-editor model tool kits that allowed activists to find their local newspaper and submit a letter online, and information regarding protest activities. Prior to the invasion of Afghanistan it sent an online petition to congress stating, "If we retaliate by bombing Kabul and kill people oppressed by the Taliban, we become like the terrorists we oppose" (MoveOn.org). In less than one week members raised $37,000 over the Internet to run an ad in *The New York Times* on December 11, 2002. It stated: "By alienating and infuriating allies through unilateral action in Iraq, the US could throw the success of the campaign against terrorism into jeopardy" (Goldberg 2002).

Once the invasion began MoveOn organized a massive transnational e-mail drive to enlist signatures for a citizens' declaration that was later published as a full page ad in *The New York Times* which read: "As a U.S.-led invasion of Iraq begins, we the undersigned citizens of many countries, reaffirm our commitment to addressing international conflicts through the rule of law and the United Nations. By joining together across countries and continents, we have emerged as a new forum for peace. As we grieve for the victims of this war, we pledge to redouble our efforts to put an end to the Bush Administration's doctrine of preemptive attack and the reckless use of military power" (MoveOn.org 2003).

Whereas MoveOn's and Win Without War's emphasis has been mainly on the United States, the online international anti-war community is indeed vast. It includes sites concerned with organizing protests outside U.S. military bases, such as Germany's Resist the War, and UK-based online groups such as the Human Shields Project, which organized to send human shields from all over the world to Iraq. The multinational effort Iraq Body Count maintains a homepage to establish an independent and comprehensive public database of civilian deaths in Iraq that have resulted directly from military actions (Webb 2003). Active soldiers and veterans have also used the Internet to exchange e-mails and participate in chat rooms that portray an alternative to the "official" version of the war in Iraq as presented in the mainstream media (Franklin and Harris 2003). Additionally, Michael Moore made public several of the letters he received via e-mail from troops in Iraq openly showcasing dissent among the ranks on his website and various listserves (Moore 2004). Between October 26th and November 1st of 2004, Alternet.org, which is a news magazine and online community based on independent journalism that advocates for a number of progressive issues, also featured a series of profiles of Iraq War veterans that exposed the real risks for troops in Iraq. These sites successfully urged veterans to form online organizations, such as Veterans for Common Sense, Operation Truth, and Iraq Veterans Against the War to campaign to bring the soldiers home.

Also through the Web, family members of troops have connected with each other, helping to foster a sense of collective identity online. Activist groups such as Bring Them Home Now, Military Families Speak Out, VoteVets, and Mothers Against War are comprised of military families, veterans, active duty personnel, and reservists. Their websites offer numerous links and news stories updating the situation of the troops on the ground and highlight the continuous threats that endanger them (Nieves 2003). These online communities also launch e-mail campaigns and strategize to organize marches and teach-ins through which the links established online can be materialized through face-to-face contact as well.

Although traditional resource mobilization theories have successfully analyzed mobilization efforts based on face-to-face contact, many contemporary social movements such as the peace movement call for an expansion of these theories to demonstrate how, through cyberactivism, individuals and coalitions foster a sense of collective identity and solidarity using new ICTs. Many scholars have argued that wired activism is becoming a significant, if not essential, repertoire for social movement actors (see Carty 2010; Smith, Costello, and Reich 2009; Jenkins 2006; Langman 2005; Nipp 2004; Pickerill 2003; Meikle 2002). Others assert that the formation of the public opinion has shifted from political institutions to the realm of communication, and more importantly from mass media to today's new networked society based on horizontal communication linkages and alternative forms of media. This allows for a counter power that can enhance alternative politics and greater participatory democracy (Castells 2007; Arsenault and Castells 2006; Habermas 1993).

Castells (2007, 2001) claims that this new type of "informational politics" has the potential to result in genuine and wired grassroots democracy among activists. Wellman (2002) concurs that ICTs enable activists to join more diverse and numerous communities than possible in the material world. Other scholars discuss how the Internet serves as a virtual public sphere that fosters fluid collective identities across various social movements, increases the visibility of opinions, and serves as avenue that can lead to actual protest and strengthen advocacy networks regardless of the fact that collective identity is established online (Smith, Costello, and Brecher 2009; Nipp 2004; Bennett 2003; Kahn and Kellner 2003). The expansion of producers, consumers, and distributers of information via ICTs and alternative media platforms such as the IMC, in addition to cell phone texting allows activists to forward messages as well as add information to the original text. This destabilizes top-down models that can enhance civic engagement on both a local and global level (Jenkins 2006; Poster 1995). The disruption of the Republican Convention in 2004 exemplifies this type of creative and bottom-up form of communication as does the overall mobilization against the war on terrorism.

The Mobilization of Resources and Social Movement Theory

Resource mobilization theory examines the tactical and strategic repertoires that activists use in specific campaigns as well as organizational dynamics, leadership, resource management, and the construction and legitimation of collective identities (Tilly 2001, 1978; McAdam, McCarthy, and Zald 1996; Gamson 1975; Oberschall 1973). Collective identity refers to the association of the goals and values of a movement with one's own, and these can be a *perception* of a shared status or relationship rather than an exclusively *concrete* one (Jasper and Polleta 2001). Employing a constructionist perspective to understand the recruitment process of new participants in collective behavior, Goodwin et al. (2001) suggest that collective identity is often rooted in feelings of compassion, indignation and moral shock—an overall shared orientation and set of grievances due to direct or indirect experiences. Collective identity helps illuminate the intermediate steps from condition to collective action and thereby refines our understanding of what links the "how" and "why" of collective behavior.

In the contemporary peace movement collective identity took on a global formation which can be understood through the lens of Keck and Sikkink's (1998) extensive work on transborder social movements. They describe such types of global mobilizing strategies as Transnational Activist Networks (TANs), through which activists in less powerful countries are linked with political actors and groups in more powerful nations that may have more leverage in influencing decisions regarding global political dynamics. TANs employ grassroots mobilization from below to try to modify the institutional forms of organized globalization from above, help cultivate movement identities that transcend nationally defined interests by petitioning for the strengthening, implementation, and monitoring of international norms, and ultimately help to build solidarity with a global emphasis (Keck and Sikkink 1998).

Dozens of NGOs and millions of citizens mobilized across borders through bottom-up networking with the realization that activists in Afghanistan and Iraq would have little success in resisting the United States' and its allies' act of war. The strategy was to work in solidarity transnationally and pressure the policy makers where they were located. The various SMOs within the peace movement used preexisting international norms to facilitate the emergence and growth of TANs and to legitimate local grievances. The various mobilizing strategies also emphasized the need for the creation of clear international standards that can be *enforced* regarding the legality of war and questioned the morality of the principles of preemptive war under the rubric of the war on terrorism. In doing so challengers sought to influence public opinion and alter the discourse of the debate by pressuring governments to act on moral principles that adhere to international standards of justice. The grassroots mobilization of the peace movement further illustrates the effectiveness of "interstitial locations" that Mann (2000) refers to, whereby marginalized citizens forge links across state boundaries and outside of the realm of institutions to the change policy from the outside.

Another key to the mobilization was the use of framing. How organizers "frame" their issues to link participants' grievances with mainstream beliefs and values is central to the formation of collective identity and solidarity (Taylor and Van Dyke 2004; Snow and Benford 1992; Snow et al. 1986). Frames are influential when organizers persuade large numbers of people that the issues they care about are urgent, that alternatives are possible, that there is a worthiness (or moral standing) of the activists' demands, and that the constituencies they seek to mobilize can be invested with agency (Tarrow and Tilly 2006). Snow et al. (1986) emphasizes the need for activists to identify problems (prognostic framing), offer solutions (diagnostic framing), and persuade people to take action (motivation framing). Social movement actors in the peace movement targeted U.S. foreign policy under the Bush Doctrine as the problem, campaigned for international standards of justice to prevail as the solution, and engaged in consciousness-raising efforts and contentious politics to expand their base of support.

Snow and Benford (1992) argue that having a "master frame" is also key to a successful campaign. This serves as a concise message that articulates grievances can also increase the effectiveness of recruitment efforts by appealing to third parties. The massive turnout for the F15 protest was in part was due to the simplicity of how the message was framed—the war was unjust—and was depicted by the rallying universal call: "The World

Says No to War." The tactics employed by challengers also illustrated the concept of frame bridging. This refers to social movement actors building on already existing norms to expand the domain to which these norms apply, and can help draw others to a cause in that the appeal for justice is put forth in a generalized sense—or an injustice frame (Ryan and Gamson 2006; White 1999; Benford and Hunt 1992; Snow and Benford 1988). The various sectors of the peace movement, in the forms of signs, slogans, petitions, mission statements, and advertisements, all incorporated a sense of injustice. By framing their concerns in moral and ethical terms these groups questioned the validity of the claims for the retaliation for the events of 9–11 and the invasion of Iraq, exposed the contradictions of government officials ignoring international norms, and subsequently challenged the framing of the issues by those promoting the war. These endeavors also demonstrate how emotion and ideology can act as pull factors as outlined by scholars such as Polletta and Jasper (2001), Klandermans (1997), Melucci (1996) and Gamson (1992).

Frame application, meaning activists' ability to appeal to deeply held values and beliefs within the general population and linking those to movement issues (Snow et al. 1986), also resonates with the mobilization efforts. Both within the United States and abroad public opinion supported letting the inspections for "weapons of mass destruction" work, and/or UN approval before the United States and its partners in the coalition invaded Iraq. For example, a poll conducted by the New York Times and CBS News showed that two out of three respondents in the United States wanted the government to wait for the UN inspections to end before it invaded, and only 31% supported using military force immediately (cbsnews.org). Internationally, in most countries (including those that were most closely aligned with the United States) over 70% of the public opposed U.S. military action against Iraq without UN approval (Pew Research Center 2003). With such strong international opposition to the war activists attempted to recruit new supporters by tapping into these common sentiments. The resistance to the Iraq invasion and war on terrorism can further be explained by new social movement theory. This paradigm holds that participants in NSMs do not necessarily seek material gain, but (among other things) attempt to challenge the diffuse notions of politics. Their participation in the political struggle is indicative of an increased consciousness that embraces a global and compassionate perspective in the form of a global identity politics whereby, through self-actualization and reflexivity, individuals embrace a sense of what unites them as human beings, of common risks and possibilities, and of mutual responsibility (Tomlinson 1999; Sklair 1998; Melucci 1996; Giddens 1991). Theories of cosmopolitanism also encapsulate this spirit by addressing the need for global strategies that include democratic global institutions based on a shared morality and politics rooted in a sense of reflexivity (see Beck 2006; Giddens 1991; Hahn 1987). International cooperation, global norms, and international institutions such as the UN figured centrally in the vision of a preferred world order by many of the organizations that mobilized against the war on terrorism.

NSM theory also postulates that in contemporary forms of struggle issues are often oriented toward control over the process of meaning, creativity of relationships, ways of defining and interpreting reality, and employing semiotic forms of resistance. Additionally, NSM actors view civil society to be a critical arena of conflict because it is in these areas where collective identities are formed and solidarity is established (Castells 2001, 1997; Gusfield 1994; Mueller 1994; Rucht 1988; Offe 1987; Touraine 1985; Melucci 1980). SMOs such as MoveOn, Why War, Win Without War, and dozens of other smaller groups established by friends and family members of 9–11 victims and U.S. soldiers mobilized to change the way the discourse of the war on terrorism was structured, questioned the social construction of reality regarding preemptive war, and established networks through diverse relationships in civil society based on a sense of collective identity.

TARGETING THE INSTITUTIONAL POLITICAL SPHERE: REVOLUTION AT THE BALLOT BOX

Despite the fact that the initial mobilization had all the components of WUNC (worthiness, unity, numbers, and commitment) as described by Tilly (2004), contentious politics by themselves were insufficient to impede the invasion or deter governments from joining the coalition of the willing. In response to the massive global protests President Bush stated he would not base policy on the opinions of a "focus group" (Stevenson 2003). Some of the most prominent nations (Britain, Spain, Italy, and Australia) that signed onto the coalition of the willing also went against the demands of the majority of their citizens. Thus, whereas resource mobilization theory is helpful in explaining how the mobilization emerged, the various tactics and strategies it used, organizational dynamics, and how a shared sense of collective identity was established, on its own it cannot adequately explain how the peace movement was ultimately able to affect state decisions regarding whether or not to join, and later to remain in or drop out of the coalition of the willing. Social movement theories that focus on institutional politics such as the political process framework are therefore a necessary accompaniment because they explore how activists can use leverage at the ballot box, manipulate divisions among elites, and take advantage of phenomena such as blowback to force their opponents to address their demands.

Political process theory can help explain *why* the mobilization was eventually successful by focusing on structural dynamics and the political and sociohistorical context within which the later victories occurred. This perspective suggests that social movements are primarily political phenomena (Amenta and Caren 2004; Kresi 2004; Kitschelt 1986; McAdam 1982; Tilly 1973). Touraine (1985) notes that actors cannot only be defined by their strategies but also by the social relationships especially the power relationships, in which these actors are involved. Thus, the ability of social movement activists to engage successfully in contentious politics relies to a large extent on political opportunity structures (POS). These are defined by Tarrow (2001) and Gamson and Meyer (1996) as institutional initiatives in the form of a shift in governance configurations toward more openness or closure of institutions and policy arenas, and/or a shift in governance culture or discourses that open spaces to make demands on governments. This can also include electoral instability and organized opposition by elites within the institutional political realm, both of which enhance the strategic position of insurgent challengers and allows them to manipulate the competition between elites (Meyer and Minkoff 2004; Meyer and Staggenborg 1998; Tarrow 1996; McAdam 1982; Jenkins and Perrow 1977; Piven and Cloward 1977).

Such conflicts may occur within or among nations, and states can become more vulnerable to activists when they are divided because it creates new spaces in which to question their agendas and create alliances with powerful actors outside the domestic political arena (Smith 2002; Marks and McAdam 1996). Therefore, within an emerging system of multi-level governance, states can at times serve as movement allies (or obstacles to movement goals) on particular issues or promote their strategic interests by aligning themselves with movement opposition to other governments' polices. Although these may only be small steps in the larger struggle, when activists effectively shape individual state decisions international campaigns have a better chance of changing international policy (Smith 2002).

President Bush's inability to garner international support from key members of the Security Council and other powerful nations to form a credible coalition of the willing resulted in a conflict between political leaders. From the onset, key Security Council members including France, Germany, China, and Russia all demanded that the UN inspectors be given more time to locate the alleged weapons of mass destruction. On the other hand, the United States, Britain, and Spain claimed that the Iraqi government was not cooperating and that an immediate assault was therefore justified. The wide international support for the U.S. attack on Afghanistan two years earlier was in large part due to the sympathy the United States enjoyed given the magnitude of the 9–11 attacks. This original outpouring of sympathy quickly faded, however, as many close allies became alienated due to the indignation that the Bush Administration displayed toward nations that were questioning its foreign policy on the issue of Iraq. For example, U.S. Defense Secretary Donald Rumsfeld referred to France and Germany as the "old" Europe when they refused to participate in the coalition, and in retaliation for Germany's reluctance to support the invasion Bush threatened to withdraw U.S. military bases from the region. Both Germany and France were also threatened with the loss of U.S. contracts for defense-related goods and services (Aguera 2003). And Bush's statements regarding the United Nations as "irrelevant" when it refused to authorize the war increased the ideological gap between the Bush Administration and the leaders of other powerful nations.

Among the countries that did participate in the coalition, almost all went against the will of their citizens. Whether their decisions were based on genuine support for U.S. policies, on fear of possible retaliation following President Bush's statement in a post 9–11 press conference that you are "either with us or with the terrorists," or on individual state decisions to pursue their own military, economic, and/or political interests are critical questions to explore (Bowley 2004). The Institute for Policy Studies (IPS) compiled an analysis of the thirty-four nations that publicly supported the United States and alleged that most were recruited through coercion, bullying, and bribery (ips-de.org). It exposed that some countries were trying to get into NATO at the time (Albania, Bulgaria, Croatia, Estonia, Latvia, Lithuania, Macedonia, Romania, Slovakia, and Slovenia) and of course were cognizant of the fact that the United States can veto nations vying for membership. Many new European countries that signed on were former Warsaw Pac nations which have historically viewed the United States as their key post Cold War international protector (Poland, Hungary, the Czech Republic, and Georgia). Other nations were receiving foreign aid from the United States and had to consider opportunities for trade and investment on the one hand, or the threat of sanctions on the other (Mexico, Turkey, Costa Rica, and the Philippines).

An underlying variable is the history of the United States retaliating against countries that vote against its interests. One of the most noted examples was when Yemen, the sole Arab country on the Council, voted against the resolution authorizing the 1991 Gulf War. A U.S. diplomat told the Yemeni ambassador, "that will be the most expensive 'no' vote you ever cast." Three days later the United States cut its entire aid budget to Yemen (Bennis 2003). The IPS analysis further noted that although the United Sates has used bribes and threats to manipulate the UN in the past, the scale of the pressure was new because governments faced such massive opposition at home. Therefore, the mobilization efforts by citizens in the countries that joined the coalition were variables that elected officials had to at least consider when deciding whether or not to participate. However, these were weighed against political and economic ramifications given their standing vis-à-vis the United States.

For what reasons governments responded to the dilemma the way they did are impossible to precisely discern, and this is consistent within much of the research regarding the impact of protest politics on policy reform. There is general agreement within the literature that the impact is dependent both on the characteristics controlled by the groups themselves and on some external to them (Dur 2008; Amenta and Caren 2004; McAdam and Su 2002; Andrews 2001; Soule et al. 1999; Giungi 1998; Minkoff 1997). Some scholars acknowledge that public opinion plays a role (Kolb 2007; Amenta, Caren, and Loasky 2005; Giungi 2004; Soule 2004; Burstein and

Linton 2002; Santoro 2002; Burstein 1998), and others focus on the importance of newly developing stages of policy making (Soule and King; 2008; Meyer and Minkoff 2004). Wright (1996) and Tarrow (2005) find that politicians' consideration of how meeting insurgents' demands will affect their electoral prospects, especially if public opinion is on the side of the challengers, to be a significant variable.

Regarding the governments that did join the coalition of the willing, it seems plausible that strategic political questions at the international level took precedence over the will of the citizens. Thus, this substantiates the proposition that external factors are an important variable regarding the relationship between protest and policy reform. However, as the political context shifted given that elections were being held in several countries whose governments supported the Bush Doctrine, activists moved their anger from the streets to the voting polls and took advantage of public opinion which sided with the challengers. They also manipulated the division among elites internationally and domestically during the electoral campaigns, which is when public opinion is most important. Thus, institutional politics worked in conjunction with protest activities, and the next section examines this dynamic more thoroughly.

Using Leverage at the Ballot Box

In several countries citizens used electoral reform to oust leaders that went against their demands in supporting the war on terrorism. An important tactic they employed was to empower politicians that supported their cause, thus enabling them to ultimately shape state decisions by questioning the legitimacy of preemptive war. Although dozens of countries decided to back Bush in the war on terrorism initially, many of these were eventually pressured to back out or experienced regime change of their own. Some of the staunchest allies, Britain's Tony Blair, Italy's Duce Silvio Berlusconi, Spain's Jose Maria Anzar, Poland's Jaroslaw Kaczynski, and Australia's John Howard all suffered losses in elections. The revolution at the ballot box was fueled by a number of factors: the initial hesitancy among citizens in most countries to support the war, protests that helped to raise consciousness regarding the reasons for the war and violations of international law, a division among elites within and across countries, and the process of blowback. Protests in several countries where political leaders originally cooperated with Bush helped lead to their defeat as activists dramatized the conflict and demanded accountability. For example, on the first anniversary of the invasion one million people protested against Berusconi's complicity with Bush and demanded the withdrawal Italian troops (Ross 2004). His challenger and now new Prime Minister, Romano Prodi, pledged to withdraw the troops in his first speech to the senate (Beeston 2005). In Poland Karzynski was replaced by Donald Rusk, who used his first speech to parliament to announce a withdrawal. In February of 2006 Blair was voted out of office. Some speculated that this was the result of his stated determination to stand "shoulder to shoulder" with Bush which put him at odds not only with British public opinion, but also with his own Labor Party (which voted against their own party), several members of his cabinet (who resigned over the Iraq issue), and members of British intelligence and the military (Kershaw 2007). Furthermore, Australian Prime Minister, John Howard, one of the first coalition partners to send troops to Iraq, was the first Australian prime minister to be voted out of parliament since 1929 as his eleven-year old government was swept from power (Fullilove 2007). The new Prime Minister, Kevin Rudd, had promised to withdraw combat troops from Iraq.

Activists also took advantage of public anxieties regarding the possibility of future terrorist attacks in order to broaden the challenge to their governments' collaboration with the United States. They argued that the possibility of blowback for participating in the coalition was putting citizens at a greater risk. The most serious episodes occurred in Spain and the United Kingdom. Three days before the Spanish general elections in March of 2004 five Madrid commuter trains were bombed, killing 190 people and injuring 1,400 (Elliot 2007). Voters elected Jose Luis Rodriguez Zapatero who fulfilled his campaign promise by swiftly removing Spain's troops from Iraq. As mentioned earlier, in March of 2003 preceding the invasion hundreds of thousands had protested in Barcelona against the government's support for the Bush Doctrine. Despite the claims by the Spanish government that the separatist Basque fraction was responsible, the official investigation by the Spanish judiciary determined the attacks were directed and carried out by an al-Qaeda-inspired terrorist cell (*The Times* 2007).

On July 7, 2005 fifty-two people were killed in London when bombs exploded on various public transportation systems, and there was another failed bombing attempt on July 21 (Cowell 2007). The London bombings also indicate that these were in retaliation for Blair's involvement in the coalition of the willing as both were linked to Islamist terrorist cells funded and aided by al-Qaeda. The Secret Organization Group of al-Qaeda of Jihad Organizing in Europe claimed to be behind the July 7 events. In a statement posted on an Islamic website, the group said the attacks were "in revenge of the massacres that Britain is committing in Iraq and Afghanistan" (hindustantimes.com). In a press conference in 2007 Bush stated that the United States and United Kingdom "are fighting these terrorists with our military in Afghanistan and Iraq and beyond so we do not have to face them in the streets of our own countries" (whitehouse.gov). Yet, the bombings in London and Madrid allowed an opportunity for the peace movement to shift the debate by arguing that citizens were increasingly vulnerable to attacks precisely *because* they were attempting to fight al-Qaeda in Afghanistan and Iraq. By framing grievances in this way it once again questioned the very notion of terrorism and challenged leaders' own use of framing in their attempt to gain public support for contributing to the U.S. invasion.

The mobilization against the war also used consciousness-raising to highlight the connection between the al-Qaeda attacks and the alliances between their leaders and the United States. Following the bombings Stop the War Coalition proclaimed that, "Every day British troops stay in Iraq the more, in the eyes of millions of people across the world, the people of this country are taken to be implicated in a murderous occupation. By associating this country with the U.S. puppet regime in Iraq, Blair increases the threat to everyone who lives there" (swp.org). The boomerang effect that joining the coalition had resulted in a change of discourse about the war and created openings for social movement actors to align themselves with domestic politicians who sided with the movement and questioned the current administrations' position regarding the war on terrorism. It also served to solidify divisions among politicians which translated into resources for social movement actors to secure their goals.

Finally, groups and individuals were able to take advantage of pragmatic failures as the war dragged on and dissatisfaction among the general public increased. The lack of an achievable goal or exit strategy, the exposure of the erroneous reports of weapons of mass destruction, the infamous "Downing Street Memo" that disclosed that a U.S. invasion of Iraq was inevitable and that the facts and intelligence were being "fixed around the policy" to invade Iraq by the Bush administration, all helped to strengthen opposition to the war. Additionally, scandals of torture in violation of international standards at the Abu Ghraib and Guantanamo Bay prisons, and the recent indictment of Blackwater Corporation for the fatal shooting of Iraqi citizens further damaged the image of the United States both domestically and abroad. These incidents helped to once again shift the discourse and framing from one based on the United States attempting to defend its citizens to one that focused on lies, deception, mishandling of the war, and disregard for the rules established under the Geneva Convention. These all helped to bolster the movement's ability to tap into and increase public opinion against the war and question U.S. foreign policy.

This chapter has highlighted how the peace movement successfully took strategic advantage of existing political opportunities, forged alliances and coalitions that expanded the movement's base of support, and expressed a clearly defined set of goals that helped to recruit new members. Through both contentious and electoral politics activists eventually came to be seen as a legitimate representative of a constituency (public opinion). This in turn affected policy-making by public officials and ultimately undermined the political institutions that supported the war effort, two important outcomes as highlighted in the literature on social movement consequences. It was the Internet that facilitated the international dimension of the struggle in terms of organizing various forms of protest, information-sharing, establishing collective identity and building solidarity, and offering counter views of preemptive war.

4 MoveOn.org and the Digital Revolution

As the previous chapters have highlighted, there is substantial agreement within the social movement literature that the Internet has certainly enhanced the capacity for political mobilization among groups and individuals. This chapter focuses on a particular online organization, MoveOn.org, which is one of the most successful public policy advocacy groups in the digital era. It works both within and outside the formal realm of institutional politics and is well known for pioneering tactics to support progressive issues, create and foster a grassroots virtual community, and raise unprecedented amounts of money to support Democratic candidates. In fact, MoveOn PAC is now one of the leading sources of financial support for Democratic candidates outside of the Party's committees.

An analysis of MoveOn is helpful in understanding how the organizational structure and tactics of e-activism allows for a new form of participatory democracy that bypasses mainstream/corporate politics and media. It does so by encouraging information sharing, dialogue, and debate among citizens both online and offline. It also suggests that the emergence of new digital technologies require further development of the concept of the "public sphere" as put forth by critical theorists such as Habermas. New social and political spaces are constantly being created through ICTs that allow for new flows of information, potentials to mobilize, and wired and concrete communities. An examination of MoveOn furthermore challenges previous research that asserts that there is little or no relationship between Internet use to obtain political information and political participation, and can address some of the fears that online organizing replaces, or is not as effective as, face-to-face organizing. To the contrary, MoveOn's mobilization endeavors represent the growing symbiotic relationship between e-activism and local organizing. Therefore, concepts such as mobilization, collective identity, and participatory democracy, originally formulated to encompass face-to-face contacts, must be rethought given the expanding cyberspace networks that fuel many contemporary forms of collective behavior.

Another compelling thing about MoveOn is that it does not fit neatly into the categories of interest group or SMO (social movement organization) that sociologists and political scientists have traditionally worked with (albeit these categories have always been messy). The fact that the entity is mainly virtual, is to a large extent member-directed, and has demonstrated an unprecedented ability to raise large sums of money from grassroots supporters make it a different kind of organization that needs theorization. It further challenges us to examine the relationship between social movements and political institutions, and raises the question as to whether this part blogosphere/part concrete and local form of organizing is a new form of collective behavior that will spread in the future.

THE HISTORY OF MOVEON

MoveOn emerged in the late 1990s and was in fact born in cyberspace via an online petition (Earl and Schussman 2008). In 1998, during the height of the Monica Lewinsky scandal, Silicon Valley computer entrepreneurs Wes Boyd and Joan Blades created an online petition that encouraged Congress to censure but not impeach President Clinton. Boyd e-mailed this to thirty friends and within two weeks more than half a million people had signed the petition (Benett and Fielding 1999). Boyd soon heard from Eli Pariser, who, after the September 11th terrorist attacks created an online petition urging moderation and restraint in responding to the terrorist acts (Pugh 2001). This site too exploded in popularity and at the suggestion of Boyd the two merged their websites and MoveOn.org was born (Markels 2003). MoveOn.org is a 501©(4) organization that focuses on education and advocacy regarding important national issues. It also has a federal Political Action Committee (MoveOn PAC). The organization currently has over five million members, and its running slogan is "Democracy in Action."

Although large in numbers, MoveOn is a quintessential grassroots mobilizing effort. According to Boyd, MoveOn tries to appeal to the highest common denominator—"ordinary, patriotic, mainstream Americans" (Leland 2003). This enables it to build coalitions across diverse constituencies which increases its ability to support a genuine kind of populism. Although MoveOn does not have systematic demographic data of its members, Boyd claims (based on anecdotal data) that most MoveOn members do not define themselves as activists but are busy professionals, and that the group has no single, easily-identifiable sectional interest or social constituency to represent (Boyd 2003). What unites MoveOn activists is support for progressive issues (for an overall view of issues see MoveOn.org/archives) and a different type of politics, and the Internet is an essential tool that allows them to stay politically connected.

The main strategy is to activate people on a few different issues at a time, often for short durations as legislative battles change, and this model allows MoveOn to play an important role as a campaign aggregator—inviting people in on a particular issue and then introducing them to additional issues, thus avoiding what Pariser calls "the single-issue balkanization of the progressive movement" (Markels 2003). MoveOn is often the first step for members into political action, and what brings them to take that step is typically an e-mail message sent from one of the organizers or forwarded from a family member, friend, or colleague. For many members contributing money toward a candidate or an advertisement in response to an e-mail is the first time they participate in politics outside of voting (Boyd 2003).

In terms of recruitment and tactics, MoveOn's success highlights the importance of flexible and contingent forms of (wired) collective identity, the blurring of the public and private spheres, and the possibility for expanded forms of communicative action. Pariser explains:

> Every member comes to us with the personal endorsement of someone they trust. Itis word-of-mouth organizing in electronic form. It has made mixing the personaland political more socially acceptable. Casually passing on a high-content message toa social acquaintance feels completely natural in a way handing someone a leaflet at acocktail party never would. The 'tell-a-friend' phenomenon is key to how organizinghappens on the Net. A small gesture to a friend can contribute to a massive multiplier effect. It is a grassroots answer to the corporate consolidation of the media. (Boyd 2003)

MoveOn is unique in that it facilities online participatory democracy through two-way forms of communication with its members. For example, the Action Forum (a cross between a blog, a discussion board, and an online rating mechanism), is perhaps one of the best examples. It allows ideas to be rated so that the organization knows what people feel most passionately about, and asks members to fill out a progress report to gauge how satisfied they are with the work MoveOn is doing in order to help plan future endeavors. Recent e-mails distributed to members have also begun directly asking them if the group should move forward on specific issues. For example, an e-mail sent out in January 2010 asked members whether or not the organization should take on immigration policy given that health care reform was being intensely debated. It specifically asked how likely they would be to sign a petition on a scale ranging from "very likely" to "not at all likely." At the end of January another e-mail queried members if comprehensive healthcare was not passed in 2010, whether they would donate to Democratic candidates in the 2010 elections. Again, participants could click on a range of choices from "definitely will" to "definitely won't," and were informed that the response would be shared with the media, the White House, and Congress. This is an extension of the Action Forum and typical of how MoveOn operates. Explaining the decision-making process, organizing director Justin Ruben states that, "MoveOn's ideological sensibility is not a product of the staff's outlook but of the views of its members . . . we believe strongly in the wisdom of crowds, giving people the ability to make choices together" (Jacobs 2005).

In addition to raising money, MoveOn's website distributes e-mail action alerts that inform its members of important current events and provides petitions and contact information of members' elected officials so that members can respond to those events. From its inception, MoveOn has embraced an approach that combines net activism with meaningful political engagement in local communities through physical attendance at rallies and fundraising events, canvassing, writing letters to newspaper editors and sending written correspondences to political leaders, making phone calls to elected officials, writing postcards to voters, distributing flyers, holding press conferences, donating money for print and television advertising, and organizing events in their communities—one of the most popular being house parties (Holland 2006).

MoveOn Campaigns and Tactics

The first campaign MoveOn was involved in was to support candidates running against impeachment backers. In 1999, in less than twelve weeks, it signed up over 500,000 supporters and received pledges of $13 million (Burress 2003). In June of that same year it set records for online fundraising by collecting more than $250,000 in five days, mostly in donations under $50 (Potter 2003). It also held an online primary, asking Democratic Party members to make donations, volunteer, and provide their e-mail address to the candidate they supported. In two days 317,000 members voted and the e-mail addresses of 140,000 supporters were passed on to the candidates' campaign teams which they could rely on for support during the primaries. Additionally, activists held a number of public meetings with members of Congress and these were used to exert lobbying pressure on behalf of a number of progressive causes (Hickey 2004). In May of 2004 its national "bake sale" (Bake Back the White House) raised over $750,000 and was supported by hundreds of thousands of volunteers (MoveOn.org 2005).

Once the Clinton impeachment trial ended MoveOn centered much of its energy on the peace movement in the wake of the 9–11 attacks. It hosted the online headquarters for the Virtual March on Washington—an act of online civil disobedience to protest the imminent invasion of Iraq. This was sponsored by the WinWithoutWar Coalition which serves as an online umbrella organization for the peace movement. Using e-mail connections to coordinate and organize a protestor base, on February 26, 2003 over 200,000 individuals signed up and made more than 400,000 phone calls and sent 100,000 faxes to every senate office in the United States with the message: DON'T ATTACK IRAQ! (MoveOn.org 2004). Every member of the U.S. Senate also received a stream of e-mails that clogged up virtual mailboxes in Washington, DC. It also worked with Win Without War to organize and publicize the international protests that took place on February 15th, which was recorded as the largest global protest ever.

Another tactic MoveOn has used repeatedly to organize around certain issues, which combines online planning with community-based organizing in the physical sphere, is candlelight vigils. The March 16th candlelight vigils, for example, involved over one million people in more than 6,000 gatherings in 130 countries and were organized in six days by MoveOn over the Internet (Hickey 2004). Its use of the online resource, Meetup, which is a peer-to-peer networking tool that allows people who are interested in a particular issue to organize meetings by voting on a time and place to meet in their local area, made the event possible.

MoveOn's fundraising ability also contributed to the anti-war effort. In less than one week members raised $37,000 over the Internet to run an advertisement in The *New York Times* on December 11, 2002. Using nonpartisan language it stated, "By alienating and infuriating allies through unilateral action in Iraq, the United States could throw the success of the campaign against terrorism into jeopardy" (*New York Times* 2002). This approach is in alignment with much of the work by framing theorists regarding the importance of linking a movement's grievances to mainstream beliefs and values to try to alter public opinion (for a more complete discussion of framing see Benford and Snow 2000; Benford 1993; Snow 1986). As the last chapter discussed, public opinion was strongly against the invasion or Iraq without UN approval and/or giving more time to look for weapons of mass destruction. In February of 2003 MoveOn solicited donations to raise $75,000 in just two hours to place an anti-war advertisement on billboards in four major American cities with a similar message (Stewart 2003).

After the invasion began, MoveOn members petitioned their congressional representatives to continue with the inspections for weapons of mass destruction. MoveOn organized a transnational e-mail drive to enlist signatures for a citizens' declaration which read: "As a U.S.-led invasion of Iraq begins, we the undersigned citizens of many countries, reaffirm our commitment to addressing international conflicts through the rule of law and the United Nations" (MoveOn.org 2003). Once again, by framing the issue as one of international concern and not one of partisan politics MoveOn was able to develop support from diverse groups. The appeal also resonated with public sentiment regarding the role of the UN. Over one million signatures were collected in less than five days and were delivered to the United Nations Security Council (Utne 2003). Signatory names and comments were also sent to the petitioners' respective congressional representatives, and on a single day 200,000 people called their representatives, and in the run-up to the Senate vote on the Iraq resolution in October of 2003 MoveOn volunteers met face to face with every U.S. senator with "Let the Inspections Work" petitions (Utne 2003).

The organization also started to more aggressively engage in political campaigns on behalf of progressive anti-war candidates once the invasion began. It urged its supporters to donate money to Democratic House and Senate members who had opposed the Iraq resolution. MoveOn commissioned a poll of sixty potential swing House districts to give Democratic challengers confidence that if they offered direct criticism of the war and a timetable to withdraw troops it would help them win (Berman 2007), and launched a project in conjunction with VoteVets.org (an organization that engages in advocacy on behalf of veterans from the Afghanistan and Iraq wars). The venture relied on "global witnessing" from soldiers returning from war (many of the vigils also used this tactic), whereby activists gave personal accounts to humanize conflict and lent credence to the activists on the basis of first-hand experience. In 2004 it raised over $30 million for Democratic candidates (MoveOn. org 2008b). Together with ACT (America Coming Together) it undertook the "Leave no Voter Behind" campaign. This used a bottom-up, person-to-person model that involved millions of ordinary citizens and precinct partners (Reilly 2004). Its Neighbor-to-Neighbor Victory Drive turned out 440,000 new voters for John Kerry and members called over 300,000 voters (MoveOn.org 2004).

However, although the organization spends large sums of money campaigning for Democrats, its relationship with the Democratic Party has been turbulent at times. This is in part due to the Party's traditional campaign style, outreach, and agenda under the DLC (Democratic Leadership Committee) which was criticized for advancing a centrist agenda and for being almost exclusively reliant on corporate fundraisers and big business. New prominent Democrats have declined ties to the committee. This includes Barack Obama who asked that his name be removed from the DLC's "100 New Democrats to Watch" (Berman 2005). All Democratic candidates spurned its annual convention in 2007, including Hillary Clinton who earlier had been one of the key leaders of the DLC (Melber 2007).

Taking advantage of the backlash against the Committee, in a December 2004 e-mail MoveOn leaders opined, "We can't afford four more years of leadership by a consulting class of professional election losers. In the last year, grassroots contributors like us gave more than $3 million to the Kerry campaign and the Democratic National Committee, and proved that the Party doesn't need corporate cash to be competitive. Now it's our party: we bought it, we own it, and we're going to take it back" (MoveOn.org 2005). By challenging the lack of leadership and creativity within the Democratic Party, it would eventually force the party to shift its practices and infrastructure toward more grassroots efforts in exchange for the organization's support.

Working with celebrities for political purposes was another innovative tactic endorsed by MoveOn. One of the group's first interactions with Hollywood came when filmmaker and co-founder of Artists United to Win Without War, Robert Greenwald, organized celebrities in opposition to the impending war in Iraq as part of the Virtual March on Washington.

MoveOn has given substantial financial support to a number of Greenwald's films and documentaries to allow for more independent and critical voices outside of mainstream and corporate-dominated media. Its website offered his "Uncovered: The Next War on Iraq" DVD as a premium to members who pledged $30 or more, and over 8,000 individuals made pledges within the first three hours. Over 2,600 members hosted screenings in their homes and at community venues, and the movie was ultimately distributed in theaters across the country (Kern 2004). A few years later MoveOn provided free copies of Greenwald's "Iraq for Sale" and "The Ground Truth" documentaries for members to show at house parties. After viewing the films attendees made phone calls and wrote letters to voters. MoveOn also helped Greenwald finance "Outfoxed: Rupert Murdoch's War on Journalism." It promoted this with house parties and took out a full-page ad in the *New York Times* declaring, "The Communists had Pravda. Republicans have Fox" (Deans 2004).

Various directors and film producers helped MoveOn construct home-made advertisements once sufficient funds were raised by its members. The "Real People" ads, for instance, were created by documentary film maker Errol Morris and featured ordinary members of the Republican Party explaining why they were crossing party lines to vote for John Kerry (Deans 2004). This was the first time both the content and the funding for an ad campaign came from the grassroots membership of an organization. The "Bush in 30 Seconds" ads challenged the Bush administration's policies and were shown during his State of the Union Address. Grammy-nominated musician Moby helped to design them and held a competition for members to submit ads and recruited a panel of celebrity judges that culminated in an awards show in New York City to raise funds for other anti-Bush television ads (Stevenson 2004).

During the 10-week "Don't Get Mad Get Even!" events preceding the 2004 election MoveOn and ACT held rallies and rock concerts that incorporated celebrity appearances by artists, authors and actors. As part of the Rock the Vote Tour they jointly held a concert in New York City right before the Republican National Convention that featured rock stars such as Bruce Springsteen, Dave Mathews Band, Pearl Jam, REM, the Dixie Chicks, Jackson Browne, and John Mellencamp. Some MoveOn members threw house parties to watch the concert, at which members wrote letters to swing state voters. Additionally, "Don't Get Mad, Get Even!" television advertisements featured celebrities/activists such as Matt Damon, Rob Reiner, Woody Harrelson, and Al Franken (Karr 2004).

MoveOn continued its grassroots mobilization during the 2006 midterm election. In an effort to regroup and rethink its strategies after Republican President George Bush was reelected in 2004, MoveOn invited members to organize and/or attend house parties to debrief the electoral process and to discuss new ideas and strategies. Its e-mail informed members that the best solutions would come not from experts and political consultants but from members thinking together. This face-to-face communication and brainstorming was supplemented by web-based organizing and mobilization. All house parties were linked by a network conference call online so attendees could view the event and participate in the discussion. What emerged was the Mandate for Change/Operation Democracy, or "people-powered" campaign (MoveOn.org 2004). The Operation Democracy field program asked volunteers to call progressive voters, house local organizers, staff support lines, recruit friends, and host or attend house parties.

MoveOn trained and supported volunteers on the ground to organize rapid responses to events and to hold news conferences, editorial board meetings, and rallies to target vulnerable Republican incumbents. To recruit the volunteers MoveOn used the organization Grassroots Campaigns to hire organizers to train and develop volunteer leaders and formed thousands of neighborhood teams and city-wide Coordinating Councils in hundreds of cities. According to a Yale University study, the emphasis on face-to-face voter mobilization through social networks increased turnout by seven percentage points (Middleton and Green 2007). Prior to the election MoveOn members held over 6,000 actions in these districts and organized 7,500 house parties (MoveOn.org 2007).

Members also donated enough money to establish the Call for Change program that used web-based tools and a call-reporting system to reach voters (Doster 2007). Once again circumventing professional pollsters, the web-based "liquid phone bank" allowed MoveOn members to call from wherever they lived into wherever they were needed within a day or two. Middleton and Green (2007) found that the phone bank was the most effective volunteer calling program ever studied, and that it increased voter turnout by almost 4%. The Call for Change initiative also included celebrities such as Stephen King who encouraged members to attend phone parties the weekend before Halloween as part of the get-out-the-vote campaign. A letter e-mailed to MoveOn members stated, "If I know anything, I know scary. And giving this president and this out-of-control Congress two more years to screw up our future is downright terrifying. Thankfully, this national nightmare is one we can end with—literally—a wake-up call" (MoveOn.org).

In anticipation of the 2006 elections MoveOn stated on its website that the strategy was to focus on the "quagmire in Iraq" and to let the voters know who was responsible for the "mess in Iraq" (MoveOn.org 2005). This was strategic posturing because by March of 2006 support for the war had fallen drastically. According to PEW Research Center, whereas in March of 2003 74% of Americans agreed that using military force was the right decision, this dropped to 43% in March of 2006. Also in March of 2003, 90% of those polled viewed the situation in Iraq as going well, in comparison to 44% three years later. Furthermore, views about keeping troops in Iraq shifted from 63% in September of 2003 to 45% in March of 2006 (PEW 2006). Thus, in synch with public opinion MoveOn pushed the issue of Iraq relentlessly during the campaign. On its website Pariser stated, "By 2006 we sensed that change was in the air. Most Americans had become fed up with the Bush Administration's disastrous Iraq policy and with the Republican Congress" (MoveOn.org 2006).

As more Democrats began to embrace MoveOn's position on Iraq the organization campaigned aggressively on behalf of anti-war candidates. It organized vigils, rallies, and other forms of direct action in addition to funding advertising campaigns—its PAC raised over $9 million for anti-war TV ads in 2005 (Holland 2006). During the 2004–2006 election cycle it raised an unprecedented $180 million and MoveOn PAC spent more than $58 million to support Democratic challengers to House and Senate victories (Federal Election Commission 2006). VoteVets and MoveOn also produced a number of advertisements during the 2006 cycle denouncing the war escalation. Members were asked to preview and vote on which videos they thought were the most compelling, and the most popular ad was shown on CNN for a week (Lou 2007).

Other creative tactics that combined bottom-up grassroots activism, popular culture and symbolic forms of resistance, and institutionalized politics included a contest asking members to pick and vote for a slogan for a poster advocating Tom Delay's dismissal that could be downloaded and hung. The Republican was accused of legal and ethical breaches of conduct, and MoveOn had also petitioned Congress to fire and him and ran TV ads supporting his dismissal. In its attack on Karl Rove, MoveOn's website provided T-shirts for sale that read, "Karl Rove ruined my country and all I got was this lousy T-shirt." Proceeds from the donation went to a fund to elect a progressive presidential candidate in 2008. The organization also provided free bumper stickers that read, "Defend America, Fire the Republicans." Boyd describes the tactics this way: "Think of it as a grassroots advertising campaign, a way to 'brand' the movement to take our country back" (Drenttel 2007).

Activists working with MoveOn during the 2006 election also helped push second-tier races into first-tier contests by identifying issues that disturbed many mainstream Americans, and articulating them in a way that resonated with potential supporters. One example is the "Red-Handed" advertisements that criticized Republican incumbents for being caught "red-handed" in accepting money from defense contractors in Iraq while voting to protect them from punishment for war profiteering and defrauding the government, in taking money from oil companies and then failing to push them to pursue clean, cheap energy sources and voting against bills that would have penalized them for price gouging, and in taking money from the pharmaceutical industry while voting to keep drug prices high for seniors (MoveOn.org 2007).

In other instances, the red-handed metaphor activated cultural-based repertoires that included humor and serious political critique. For example, displaying giant foam red hands and signs, MoveOn members followed their representatives to town hall meetings, appearances, and fundraisers questioning their allegiance to special interests. In Virginia Beach, members attended every "Coffee with Thelma" event that Representative Drake held to ask questions about her allegiance to special interests. In Louisville, Kentucky, members rallied at a gas station to tell voters about Representative Ann Northup's ties to big oil with flyers describing war profiteering. Members in Fayetteville, North Carolina, attended a defense contractor tradeshow that Representative Robin Hayes sponsored. During this campaign alone local media wrote over 2,000 stories about MoveOn's actions (MoveOn.org 2008), and of the nine long shot races members targeted, five won. However, two House Republicans that survived the MoveOn offensive were Rep. Deborah Pryce (OH) and Rep. Thelma Drake (VA). Drake won a second term with 51% of the vote. She withstood the $529,535 raised by MoveOn, which spent more money trying to defeat her than on any other incumbent (the *New York Times* listed the "Red-Handed" ads against Rep. Drake as one of the seven most effective that election cycle) (MoveOn.org 2006). As an overall tally, in 2006 Democrats supported by MoveOn lost four and won eighteen races and helped build a Senate Democratic majority (Center for Responsive Politics 2006).

The red-handed campaign represents what MoveOn does best—framing issues in a way that resonates with voters and taps into their frustration while using humorous and innovative techniques. The organization has successfully branded dissent through succinct framing of issues, grabbed media attention through creative forms of activism, and built collective identity among members through many of these tactics. Its success at harnessing popular entertainment to get alternative voices heard, whether in the form of rock concerts, fundraisers, Bush-bashing ads, publicity stunts, or supporting alternative forms of media, and doing this jointly with representatives of the artistic community, is something MoveOn has excelled at. Boyd explains, "We believe in big cultural messages; we believe that politics should be something that is part of mass culture" (Brownstein 2004).

In June of 2008 MoveOn, for the first time ever, endorsed a candidate when Barack Obama received 70% of the vote through an e-mail straw poll of its members. It distributed several e-mails to supporters after the endorsement encouraging them to donate money, participate in get-out-the-vote activities, and talk to co-workers, friends and family members about the upcoming election. In 2008 its overall independent expenditures totaled $5,202,335 for Democrats and $1,447,000 against Republicans (Center for Responsive Politics 2008). After the election MoveOn reported that nearly one million volunteers put in over 20,841,507 hours of their time to canvass, register voters, and make 2.6 million get-out-the-vote calls (MoveOn.org 2008).

UPDATING SOCIAL MOVEMENT THEORIES TO ACCOUNT FOR THE DIGITAL REVOLUTION

The literature on NSMs suggests that organizational features of contemporary social movements are distinct from traditional forms of organization because they are constituted by loosely articulated networks that permit multiple memberships and part-time participation, there is little if any distinction between leaders and rank-and-file members, members and nonmembers, and private and public roles (Castells 1997; Gusfiled 1994; Mueller 1994; Offe 1985). MoveOn embodies each of these through tools such as the Action Forum, Meetup, the forwarding of e-mails, and e-mails from staff that try to gauge the level of interest and support for various causes among members. Online organizations such as MoveOn are also changing the way information is sent, received, and accessed and represent a more pluralistic, fluid, and issue-oriented group politics. They operate at a grassroots level working outside of state-regulated and corporate-dominated media. Through quick and innovative actions, mediated across electronic networks, MoveOn allows for new forms communicative action that assists in recruitment efforts and can result in concrete forms of mobilization.

Habermas' (1993, 1989) attention is on how citizens can form alliances to reestablish defense of the public sphere and participatory democracy. The public sphere refers to the space that mediates between the private sphere and that of public authority; areas of social life where citizens can freely and face-to-face discuss and debate societal concerns that are important to them. Melucci (1996) refers to this as an "intermediate public space" where social movement actors can politicize civil society by making society hear their messages and which can then enter the process of political articulation. As originally depicted, the public sphere consisted of information distributors such as print media as well as physical social areas. Habermas contends, however, that this realm has been colonized as relationships are increasingly mediated by money and power, and entrenched political parties and interest groups substitute for participatory democracy (1981). He also claims that with the rise of late capitalism, the culture industries, and the power of corporations in public life citizens have become passive consumers of goods, services, political administration, and spectacle and the result is a decline in democracy, individuality and freedom (1989). Public opinion, he argues, is now administered by political, economic, and media elites which mediate public opinion as part of social control.

Thus, public opinion shifts from one based on the outcome of debate, discussion, and reflection (what he refers to as communicative action) to the manufactured opinion of polls or media experts and political consulting agencies. The function of the media has therefore been transformed from facilitating an exchange of ideas and debate within the public sphere into shaping, constructing, and limiting public discourse to those themes validated and approved by media corporations. However, he is optimistic about the possibility of the revitalization of the public sphere—one that transcends geographically boundaries to embrace democracy based on a political community that can collectively define its political will and implement it. This new political system requires an activist public sphere where matters of common interest and political issues can be discussed and the force of public opinion can influence the decision-making process. Yet, his theory stops short of assessing how technological and media advances may bring this to fruition.

Theories of new ICTs can help fill this void. Many scholars have noted that the production, sharing, and consumption of ideas and information has shifted from the uni-directional flow of information (as it existed under the controlled and centralized nature of broadcast TV and mainstream media) toward new forms of media that provide peer-to-peer sharing and horizontal forms of communication. This allows for a growing potential for a more informed citizenry and novel forms of activism (Carty 2009; Jenkins 2006; Langman 2005; Kellner 2004; Castells 2001; Diani 2000). There is also agreement that because information has become a crucial resource in modern society, collective action designed to change the ways in which public discourse is structured is essential (Castells 2007, 2001; Harvey 1998).

MoveOn is typical of what Castells (2001) refers to as a new type of "informational politics" in which electronic media become the space of politics by framing processes, messages, and outcomes and results in a new kind of civil society based on what he calls the "electronic grassrooting of democracy." Social agency, according to him, is now expressed through practices of identity politics because the diffusion of new ITCs has promoted the development of horizontal networks of interactive communication. Others have argued that the Internet serves as a medium through which collective identity is supported because it can provide visibility of opinions and opportunities not allowed for in mainstream media and traditional forms of communication. It also allows for participants to comment on and/or pass along information through virtual public spheres (Jenkins 2006; Van Aelst and Walgrave 2003; Diani 2000; Kollock and Smith 1999; Pliskin and Romm 1997).

Scholars have also depicted how through the use of ICTs members are organized through online non-hierarchical channels that are geographically and/or socially diverse, but who share common interests (Garrett 2006; Hampton 2003; McCaughney and Ayers 2000; Arquilla and Ronfledt 2001; Brainard and Siplon 2000; Wellman 2000). This organizational structure and agenda supports Bimber's (2003) view of the democratizing process of collective and political action in that the boundaries of online groups are porous and decision-making collaborative. Ultimately, he suggests, this results in more self-governing types of organization. Kahn and Kellner's (2003) concept of "post-subcultures," defined as online interpersonal networks of discussion and debate that create spaces for the democratic construction, negotiation, and articulation of new constellations of project identities is also evident in the organizational structure and tools used by MoveOn.

Perhaps most importantly, an examination of MoveOn challenges some assumptions about potential negative effects of cyberactivism and online communication. Some research has contended that virtual social relations in cyberspace are not a substitute for more traditional forms of community, protest, and collective identity due to a lack of interpersonal ties that provide the basis for the consistency of collective identities and ability to mobilize new members (Pickerill 2003; Kraut et al. 1998). Additionally, studies express a concern regarding diminished membership in civic and political organizations due to online interaction or exposure to mass media in general (Nie and Erbring 2000; Putnam 2000). As MoveOn illustrates, however, new digital network configurations can facilitate permanent campaigns and the growth of broad networks despite relatively weak social identity and ideology ties, thus supporting the findings of Bennett (2003) and Van Aelst and Walgrave (2003).

This case study also illuminates how online organizing and networking often leads to political activism in "real" communities as web-based ties and social relations often spill over into the material world, and organizers can then mobilize these groups to strengthen advocacy networks. This adds credence to research that finds community-based activism closely related to, or initiated by online activism and organizing (Jenkins 2006; Nipp 2004; Bennett 2003). The tactical innovation used by MoveOn via electronic mediums expands the nature of participatory democracy by combining material and virtual forms of political activity that in the past would have been perceived as distinct organizational types.

An analysis of MoveOn further questions suggestions that there is little or no relationship between Internet use to obtain political information and political activity and that the tendency among people to seek out information that will only be relevant to them, making recruitment efforts difficult for social movement actors (Bimber and Davis 2001; Bimber 1998). The "tell a friend" phenomenon and forwarding of e-mails, and the resulting interest of the recipient on the basis of trust of the source (be it a member's trust in the overall mission of MoveOn or that of a non-member based on the trust of the sender of a forwarded e-mail), calls for caution in assuming these two claims. It also advocates the need for an expanded conceptualization of obtaining information to include the *reception* of information electronically from trusted sources. Although people may be selective in what they seek out, when information is sent electronically from a source one confides in this it may broaden Internet-users' exposure to social or political issues.

Similarly, contentions that online interaction is mainly composed of like-minded people who are often predisposed to issues that draw Internet users to various sites (Jordan 2001; Diani 2000) are suspect. In the case of MoveOn, members receive constant e-mails across a wide variety of issues, and many potentially pertain to issues they are not familiar with or well-informed about; from the invasion of Iraq, to staff cuts at major newspapers, to wiretapping of U.S. citizens without warrants, to the inept response to Hurricane Katrina, to drilling in the Arctic, to the privatization of social security, etc., etc. This process of issue-aggregator sets MoveOn apart from previous forms of mobilization, recruitment, and online activism as members and citizens who are recipients of e-mails may not have been predisposed to the issues beforehand.

Although an analysis of MoveOn provides many promising liberating potentials of the Internet, there a few caveats that deflate an exclusively celebratory perspective. First, items on the Action Forum are included at the directors' discretion. This ultimately represents a top-down approach, and certain items that are of concern to members are sometimes left out. For example, many groups and individuals complained that the troop resurgence in Afghanistan, as proposed by Obama, was not included as an item to rank on one of the recent lists. Second, although the directors of MoveOn send out a plethora of e-mails and encourage them to be forwarded to an acquaintance, the organization typically does not responded to e-mails from its members (the author has sent numerous e-mails and has never received a response). Relatedly, there is little transparency regarding how directors respond to members' feedback. These issues regarding the *anti-democratic* nature of the Internet need further theorization and will be revisited in the next chapter.

How to Conceptualize MoveOn: Electronic SMO or Something New?

MoveOn's fluctuation between institutional and extra-institutional politics, and its vacillating relationship to the Democratic Party sometimes blurs its identity and status and poses a series of interesting questions. Political scientists and sociologists have long grappled with the entangled relationship between political parties, independent political groups, social movement actors, and dissident groups that run identified candidates for office (Mikoff 1994; Lucardie 2000; Amenta and Ilyan 1999; Buton, Wald, and Rienzo 1999). Whereas parties are firmly established in the realm of institutionalized politics, the status of, and tactics used by, SMOs, interest groups, and other dissident groups are more complicated. The latter three provide alternative modes of interest aggregation and articulation to citizens, and have become a serious competitor to political parties for support bases (Diamond and Gunther 2001), and thus need to be theorized both in their own right and in relation to other actors.

Although SMOs overlap to some degree with interest groups, there are a few key distinctions (as outlined by Snow et al. 1986). First, interest groups are generally defined in relation to the government and are regarded as legitimate actors within the polity that have access to powerful decision makers. The interests of social movements, on the other hand, extend to other extra-institutional spheres and authorities. Second, even when social movements are oriented to the polity or state, their standing is different because they typically remain outside of the polity because they rarely have the same degree of access to, or recognition among, political authorities. Third, interest groups pursue their collective objectives mainly through institutionalized means such as lobbying, fundraising and internal party organizing whereas social movement actors pursue their collective ends via and the use of contentious politics.

Although these distinctions hold true in a general sense, recent literature has noted that the line between contentious and electoral politics is becoming progressively more difficult to discern as groups shift from one to the other according to the political opportunity. Also, coalitions among groups working within the institutional arena and groups protesting outside are often part of the same movement (Sikkink 2005; Soule and Earl 2005; Tarrow 2005; Tarrow and Tilly 2001). The emergence of groups like MoveOn highlight the difficulty in trying to decipher the differences. The organization does not fit neatly into the category of interest group (its issues are widespread and it often works outside of the polity), nor can it be classified as an SMO in the traditional sense because it does not represent a particular "social movement" per se. In some ways MoveOn is *similar* to an SMO in its attempt to construct a progressive ideology, provide an institutional structure that serves to organize resources, and at times engage in extra-institutional and disruptive tactics. It also operates in a way that, as Goldstone (2003) outlines, SMOs have done so in the past: embracing civil society activism to promote socio-political awareness and change, deepening democratic spaces, increasing accountability among elected officials, and leading political parties in a new direction.

Over the past several years MoveOn has shifted more toward working within the formal political realm, and thus political process theory can help shed light on how to theorize the novelty of its status. Much of the research suggests that political opportunity structures can be viewed, at times, as specifically issue-oriented or constituency-specific as social movement actors attempt to affect policy given signals in the political environment (Meyer 2006; Amenta and Caren 2004; Meyer and Minkoff 2004; Sanotoro 2002; Tarrow 1998). Public opinion is one such signal that activists respond to and use to their advantage when politicians are reluctant to address their demands (Rojas 2006; Soule and Olzak 2004; Burstein and Linton 2002). MoveOn has been able to successfully respond to public sentiments among its members and citizens in general with its issue-specific campaigns.

Tarrow (2005) contends that often the inability or unwillingness of politicians or political parties to take stands on contentious issues provides a space for organizations of civil society as brokers outside the formal institutional framework of the political system. He argues that election years often shift the relationship between political parties and social movement activists as politicians tend to be more attuned to public opinion, and therefore more willing to listen to alternative views. Similar research illustrates that there a number of variables that politicians consider when an SMO makes demands: how meeting the organization's demands will affect the officials' electoral prospects; how many members the organization has; its organization strength; whether the group can mobilize its members to vote; and whether the organization can provide resources such as money, campaign workers, and access to media (Wright 1996; Soule and Olzak 2004; McCammon et al. 2001). As the first half of the chapter depicted, MoveOn qualifies in each of the above factors. Overall, MoveOn enlarged the sphere of public discourse; drew rank-and-file citizens into the formal realm of politics through canvassing, fundraising, and voting, and augmented accountability among politicians.

The political process model provides an analytical framework within which to understand MoveOn's position in relation to the Democratic Party and its ability to take advantage of divisions among elites. The splintering within the Democratic Party, resulting mainly from the backlash against the DLC leadership, allowed MoveOn to fill an important political void and increase its leverage vis-à-vis the Party. It influenced those within the polity to adapt their practices toward more grassroots efforts in exchange for the organization's support (this was mostly clearly illustrated during 2008 presidential election and will be discussed in detail in the following chapter). The organization not only solidified its position due to conflict among party leaders but proactively tried to create conflicts. For example, by making the issue of the invasion of Iraq during the 2006 election it took an active role in aiding anti-war candidate Ned Lamont who was trying to unseat Senator Joseph Lieberman of Connecticut, then a Democrat supporting the war effort (Healey 2006). In anticipation of the 2008 elections, MoveOn asked its members if they should organize potential primary challengers against Democrats who were not tough on the war in Iraq and responding to a "yes" vote did so. It also ran a TV campaign against Washington Democratic Rep. Brian Baird after he announced the troop surge may be achieving important military gains.

In conclusion, although MoveOn technically doesn't qualify as an SMO (in terms of its status), it is illustrative of the complexity in trying to distinguish between interest groups and SMOs as its tactics resemble those of both. MoveOn perhaps can best be conceptualized as a hybrid in terms of its status (part insider/part outsider) and a chameleon in terms of tactics (part disruptive yet much more engaged in the institutionalized side of the continuum of contentious/institutional politics). Although it emerged as a dissident organization, it eventually evolved into more of a political advocacy group that supports pinpointed candidates for office, and operates in an ad hoc fashion without a traditional organizational structure. Thus, it can also be characterized as what some scholars refer to as a "social movement community" (Wollenberg et al. 2006; Polleta and Jasper 2001; Staggenborg 1998; Beuchler 1993).

The advocacy group has garnered available resources, people, and computer skills to increase socio-political awareness, influence public opinion, mobilize citizens and network with other SMOs, and help elect progressive candidates. It has used tactical innovation to tap into submerged networks that have become a vehicle for the emergence and articulation of Internet-mediated forms of civic engagement. By combining a flexible entrepreneurial style with a strong ethic of listening to its members, it has built a responsive and populist virtual community, revitalizing and deepening grassroots community-based mobilization across the dimensions of virtual and local space. It also demonstrates that although the Internet has not replaced traditional models of organizing, nor replaced activism in the material, it has altered the contours of mobilizing strategies and participatory democracy in important ways and that variate along the typical spectrum of contentious politics and protest. Thus, the often perceived zero-sum game between new and old activism is a false dichotomy because, as MoveOn depicts, online and offline activism often reinforce each other. Ultimately, what makes it intriguing is how its online operations allow it to straddle not only the virtual/material sphere in terms of collective identity, organization, and mobilization, but also variate along the spectrum of SMO and interest group.

The question of whether or not this model can be replicated, and how to best conceptualize and theorize new online organizations, opens up areas for future research. Indeed, we are beginning to see the replication of this model used for political ends. As this book goes to press, little-known Republican Scott Brown ran a grassroots campaign in Massachusetts to win the vacated seat by Ted Kennedy in a special election. This Seat had been held by Democrats since 1978. He won with the help of a Tea Party organized online "money bomb" (Tea Party activists raised over one million dollars online in twenty-four hours) and a get-out-the-vote campaign, both borrowed from MoveOn (Stauber 2010). In fact, Freedom Works and other groups behind the Tea Party populists have long claimed that they would create the Right's equivalent of MoveOn, and have successfully tapped into the disillusionment with Obama and the Democratic Party the way that Obama and MoveOn did with the frustration of Democrats with their Party. And, we can raise a similar issue as to how to conceptualize the Tea Party populists—SMO, interest group, or somewhere in between?

5 The 2008 U.S. Presidential Election and Youth Activism
Digital Technologies as Grassroots Empowerment or Elite Control?

The 2008 U.S. presidential election was exceptional for a few reasons. The two most notable perhaps were that for the first time an African American was voted into office, and it was also arguably the first "social media" election given the role of the Internet and other new digital technologies. For example, 39% of Americans said they had watched online political videos (candidate debates, speeches, and announcements), triple the rate from 2004, and 46% reported that they used the Internet, e-mail, and texting to get news about the campaign, share their views, and mobilize others (Smith and Rainie 2008). The proportion of Americans who stated that they regularly learned about the campaign from the Internet more than doubled since 2000—from 9% to 24%, and 42% of those 18–29 reported that they learned about the campaign from the Internet, which was triple the percentage for any news source (Kohut 2008). There was also a significant revival of the youth vote, as the 18–29 block turned out in the highest numbers in over thirty-five years. Citizens within this age group went to the polls in numbers exceeding any election since 1972, and 66% of them voted for Obama (Drehle 2008). Whereas overall Democratic turnout increased 90% from 2004, the number of young Democrats participating soared 135% (Von Drehle 2008).

There was also a dramatic increase in volunteerism in political campaigns among youth. A CBS-MTV poll found that one quarter of voters under thirty had worked on a campaign, joined a political club, or attended a political rally (Lawrence 2008). Many of these worked for the Obama campaign which not only targeted young voters, but also *seemingly* ran a decentralized, transparent, and bottom-up campaign that allowed supporters to participate in ways they had not been able to in previous elections. It achieved this by providing infrastructure, digital technologies, training, and tools to communicate and mobilize supporters both virtually and face-to-face.

As noted in the previous chapters, ICTs have revolutionized the way collective political and social actions are organized (both online and offline), how volunteers are amassed, funds are raised, and messages honed and delivered. Whereas these chapters focused mostly on contentious politics and/or political advocacy groups, this one analyzes how grassroots efforts, enabled by emerging digital technologies, in some ways allows political candidates to subvert the traditional professional campaign model and skirt mainstream media. However, it also challenges the assumption in much of the literature that digital media has *unproblematically* shifted the balance of power in terms of organization and mobilization away from the professional model toward grassroots organizing.

Contrary to many popular accounts that portrayed Obama's strategy as relying almost exclusively on a volunteer-driven and bottom up organizing campaign, a more critical gaze reveals that the campaign was actually very much structured within a hierarchal system that was used to further institutionalized political ends. During the Obama campaign citizens were *selected* as the targets of political communication, and interactivity was structured from *top down* through the work of political intermediaries, i.e., professional campaign consultants. Thus, this chapter also explores how the complex combination of new digital media/technologies and old gate keepers affects citizen engagement, ultimately having both liberating potentials and limiting effects.

REVIVAL OF THE YOUTH VOTE AND NEW DIGITAL TECHNOLOGIES

Although young citizens (18–29) represent one of the largest voting blocs, over the past three and a half decades this segment of the population has tended to vote at low rates. Whereas in 1972 50.3% of all eligible young people voted, this dipped to 41% in 2000. Between 2000 and 2008 there was an 11% increase in youth voter turnout; the rate was 41%, 48%, and 52% respectively for the 2000, 2004, and 2008 elections (Center for Information and Research on Civic Learning and Engagement 2008). An estimated twenty-three million young Americans under the age of thirty voted in the 2008 presidential election, and this age group constituted 18% of all voters (Tirsch 2008). Also, young people have been involved in public service more than ever. The volunteer rate for sixteen to twenty-four year olds, for example, was 21.9% in 2008, and according to the Higher Education Research Institute, in that same year 69.7% of young citizens agreed with the statement: "it is essential to help other people in need"—the highest rate since 1970 (Lui et al. 2009). The below chart traces the youth vote from 1972 to 2008 for both Democrats and Republicans.

In the past two presidential elections it was primarily the Democrats that benefited from the youth vote. In 2004 the 18–29 block was the only demographic to break for Kerry, who got 54% of the vote versus George Bush's 44% (Goldberg 2008). During that election young voters were targeted not so much by politicians but by grassroots advocacy groups, and much of it in the form of entertainment (this was addressed in Chapter 4).

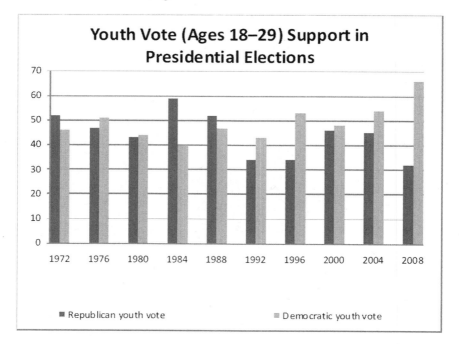

Figure 5.1   Youth-vote support (age 18–29) in professional elections.

Although these efforts effectively got young people to the polls, similar to previous presidential campaigns, there was no incentive or real opportunity for them to volunteer and work within the campaigns. This changed in 2008 as campaigns tapped into new digital technologies where young citizens were gathering to find information, communicate, and network.

Social networking sites were not available in 2004, but were crucial in terms of reaching young voters in 2008. At the time of the 2008 election, two-thirds of Internet users under the age of thirty had a social networking profile, and half of those used social networking sites to get or share information regarding the campaign and to seek out ways to participate (Aun 2007). Overall, 27% of those ages 18–24 had retrieved campaign information from social networking sites, whereas just 4% of Americans in their thirties, and 1% of those ages forty and older got news about the campaign that way (Kohut 2008). Among respondents under the age of thirty, 8% said they signed up as a "friend" of one of the candidates on a site, compared to 3% for those 30–39 (Kohut 2008). Additionally, according to Nielsen/Net Ratings report, MySpace users between eighteen and twenty-four were nearly three times more likely than average Web users to interact online with a public official or candidate. They were also 42% more likely to view online videos that related to politics or public affairs, and 35% more likely to listen to online audio related to political and public affairs (Aun 2007).

It was the Obama campaign that best mined the energy of youth participation in public service and their political activity via new technologies (74% of wired Obama supporters got political news and information online), and perfected ways of reaching and incorporating youth into its mobilization efforts (Goldberg 2008). Obama's message of hope and change also targeted young voters at a time when public service among youth was at an all time high, and his use of the Internet and social media platforms far outranked his contenders. Specifically, his campaign turned out voters twenty-five and younger (many first time voters) in record numbers. And, he was able to do it across party lines as there was united support among young voters for him regardless of their political affiliation. For example, whereas 33% of young voters self-identified as "Democrat," 54% voted for Obama, and voters under twenty-five preferred him over the next-closest competitor by more than four to one (Drehle 2008).

The Obama staff purposefully tried to find, organize, and energize supporters in a way that enabled them to create a space outside of things they were disillusioned with: the mass media, lobbyists, and the rituals of institutional politics (Howe and Strauss 2008). To do so, it organized teams of volunteers across the United States and created training spaces for them to participate in and learn about grassroots political mobilization. It also aligned itself with other political advocacy groups and emulated some of their formulas that had proven successful in the past, and most prominently MoveOn.org. In fact, Obama recognized the important role that MoveOn played throughout his campaign after his victory declaring, "In just a few years, the members of MoveOn have once again demonstrated that real change comes not from the top-down but from the bottom-up. . . . It shows what Americans can achieve when we come together in a grassroots movement for change. You and millions of others working through MoveOn have helped change the way politics works in this country" (MoveOn.org 2008).

On the other hand, his opponent, Republican John McCain, had a message that tended to support the status quo, and his use of digital technologies was very limited in comparison to Obama's. Whereas Obama's Vote-for-Change.com website provided voter registration information to potential voters and dedicated a section specifically targeting young potential voters, McCain's website was the only one that did not have a section devoted to addressing the youth vote. Furthermore, according to a Gallup Poll, Americans under thirty were contacted by the Obama campaign at nearly twice the rate as by the McCain campaign; 31% versus 16% (www.gallup.com 2008). The two tables below compare Obama's and McCain's campaign efforts during the general election, both online and offline.

Table 5.1   Obama Versus McCain Campaign Activity and Support

Campaign activity/support	Barack Obama	John McCain
Number of Facebook friends on Election Day	2,397,253	622,860
Change in the number of Facebook friends since Election Day (as of Nov. 8)	+472,535	-2,732
Number of unique visitors to the campaign website for the week ending Nov. 1	4, 851,069	1,464,544
Number of online videos mentioning the candidate uploaded across 200 platforms	104,454	64,092
Number of views of those videoss	889 million	554 million
Number of campaign-made videos posted to YouTube	1,822	330
Total amount of time people spent watching each campaign's videos, as of Oct. 23	14.6 million hours	488,000 hours
Cost of Equivalent purchase of 30-second TV ads	$46.9 million	$1.5 million
Contributions to the candidate, including public financing, as of Oct. 15	$639 million	$360 million
Number of Twitter followers	125,639	5,319
Number of blog posts using the phrase "voting for____"	79,613	42,093
Number of references to the campaign's voter contact operation on Google	479,000	325
Number of direct links to the campaign's voter contact tool	475	18
Percentage of voters who said they received calls or visits on behalf of the campaign	26	19

Source: Rasiej and Sifry, Personal Democracy Forum's techPresident.com blog

POLITICAL CAMPAIGNING, THE INTERNET, AND NEW MEDIA PLATFORMS

Similar to the organizational efforts that have embraced contentious politics, the institutional political sphere has also witnessed a vast expansion of online organization and mobilization over the past decade. Political campaigning on the Web began in 1996 as a number of candidates created relatively simple websites which provided campaign material electronically,

Table 5.2   Online Activity Comparing Obama and McCain

Virtual Interactivity Comparing Obama and McCain

Obama 2x more	Obama 4x more	Obama 5x more	Obama 10x more
Web Site Traffic	YouTube viewers	Facebook friends	Online Staff

Source: Edelman 2009

and that would typically have been printed on leaflets. Thus, they were essentially electronic flyers. By 2000 candidates expanded Web pages by encouraging visitors to their sites to make donations and view additional information such as upcoming events. However, it was in 2004 that the Internet became an integral component of political campaigning as citizens increasingly were taking advantage of new ICTS to gain knowledge of the candidates and participate in the campaigns. During the 2004 election 37% of all Americans, and 61% of those online, used the Internet to get political news and information, discuss candidates, volunteer, or give contributions to candidates (Rainie et. al. 2005). There was also a turn toward greater citizen-to-candidate and citizen-to-citizen interactivity through blogs, online discussion forums, and other ICTs.

It was the 2004 Howard Dean campaign (who ultimately lost the Democratic nomination to John Kerry) that pioneered new ways of engaging supporters online. Through a network of websites and blogs he and his team, led by campaign manager Joe Trippi, created a dedicated Internet following that helped him lead all Democratic candidates in fundraising (Rice 2003). Over the course of the primaries 280,000 supporters contributed $40 million to the campaign—a Democratic Party primaries record (Singel 2004). Dean was also the first presidential candidate to create a blog as part of his communication strategy, soon followed by other top Democrat contenders such as John Edwards and John Kerry, and George Bush on the Republican side. The campaign was also adept at linking with other political groups and positioning itself in existing online political weblogs, most notably the Daily Kos. Additionally, Dean was the first to use the Internet to organize thousands of volunteers who canvassed in door-to-door activities, letter-writing campaigns, and the distribution of flyers (Wolf 2004).

The driving force behind the campaign was the use of peer-to-peer politics through manual referral and automated linking technologies. Perhaps most effective was the use of Meetup.com (an Internet tool that allows individuals to connect virtually in order to find people in their local communities). In March of 2003 there were seventy-nine Meetups in fourteen cities; by the end of the year the Dean group on Meetup had 140,000 members and 800 meetings were held across the country in December (Dodson and Hammersley 2003). Acknowledging the significance of the bottom-up, grassroots and Web-based activism Dean explained, "They built our organization for us before we had an organization" (Wolf 2004).

Dean's use of Meetups, blogger networks, viral house meetings, discussion forums, and online donation drives went beyond the repertoires used in previous U.S. elections. However, the grassroots and decentralized network of supporters never merged with the traditional Democratic power structure or leadership (of which Dean was very critical of), and Dean Headquarters did not play a role in regulating the various networks (Hindman 2005). The technology at that time did not allow the campaign to retain control over the Meetups, which were left up to Internet activists and local organizers. These two shortcomings were circumvented by Obama in 2008, whose campaign perfected and far surpassed Dean's innovative use of the Internet.

By 2008 all candidates were using digital forms of technology extensively. The utilization of blogs, social networks, text messaging, e-mail lists, candidate's Web pages, social networking sites, and photo and video sharing sites were harnessed to reach, inform, and mobilize supporters. All candidates had thorough Web strategies, Web teams, and multiple points of presence on-line, including Facebook and MySpace (Hesseldahl et. al 2008). The utilization of these new media platforms were crucial in targeting the youth voting block, which increasingly communicates digitally through social networks. The Pew Internet and American Life Project, for example, found that 27% of voters under the age of thirty received information about the campaign and the candidates from social networking sites, and 22% said that they would not have been as involved in the campaign if not for the Internet (Kohut 2008).

Candidates also used YouTube as a way to connect with the youth vote. Seven of the sixteen candidates who ran for the presidency announced their candidacies on YouTube and all opened YouTube accounts. In preparation for the election, YouTube created YouChoose, a section of the site devoted to the posting of videos from candidates in the form of speeches and ads (Rawlinson 2008). It also provided a platform for people to engage in dialogue with candidates and each other through the use of features such as video responses, text comments, and ratings. MySpace also hosted online town halls with presidential candidates on various colleges and universities whereby members of MySpace could watch the webcast and submit questions both in person and over the Web. It also launched a month pre-primary straw poll that allowed MySpace users to vote on candidates, and its Impact channel housed all of the presidential candidates' official MySpace pages (Aun 2007).

Despite the increasing dependency on digital technologies throughout the 2008 election, new media did not completely eclipse or replace traditional sources, but rather the two merged. For example, ABC struck a partnership with Facebook to provide political and debate information for the 2008 election. CNN, YouTube, and MySpace teamed with MTV to present a presidential dialogue series featuring presidential hopefuls (Whitney 2008). MoveOn partnered with air America Radio to bring the first ever virtual town hall meeting for the 2008 Democratic presidential candidates. The venue of the Democratic Presidential debates, sponsored by CNN, requested that people submit questions through YouTube to be broadcast and answered on CNN (Heffernan 2008). According to Nielsen Media Research (2007), the July 2008 broadcast delivered a higher viewership among citizens 18–30 than any other debate in cable history. And when Obama was sworn into office in February of 2009, nearly twenty-seven million people watched the streaming video on CNN.com, a record-setting number. All of these represent a hybrid of new media and old gatekeepers and one which has clearly impacted political campaigning and ways to reach young voters.

The Obama Campaign

The Obama campaign, like the Dean campaign which preceded it, illustrates how new digital networks are reworking fundamental relationships between citizens and candidates. Replicating what Dean and MoveOn had done in earlier elections, Obama used the Internet extensively to fundraise and recruit. Wired Obama voters were more than twice as likely to contribute money (15% vs. 6%) and to sign up for campaign-related volunteer activities (11% vs. 4%) than offline supporters (Smith 2009). Overall, three million donors made a total of 6.5 million donations online, adding up to more than $500 million, and of those six million were in increments of $100 or less with the average being $80 total (Vargas 2008). Also following the lead of MoveOn and the Dean campaign, the Obama team leveraged new digital technologies to provide citizens access to resources usually reserved for professional campaign operatives. It employed a bottom-up grassroots approach to bypass professional pollsters as virtual phone banks, accessed through Obama's official website, allowed volunteers to sign in online, receive a list of phone numbers, and make calls from home. Volunteers made three million calls were made in the final four days of the campaign alone using the virtual phone-banking platform (Liasson 2008).

However, going beyond these efforts, the Obama campaign also built a powerful political infrastructure that relied heavily on social-networking sites. The online organizing began in earnest during the primaries when Obama hired Joe Rospars (who had worked on Dean's campaign in 2004) to be his online director, and Facebook co-founder, Chris Hughes. This "New Media Division" of the campaign created Obama's own social networking site, myBarackObama.com (MyBO), in addition to managing the candidate's presence on sites including Facebook, MySpace, and YouTube (Sifry 2008). The goal on all of the social networking sites was to use each supporter's profile page as a communications hub within that supporter's own social circle, building up volunteers and donors friend-to-friend. The campaign relied on the idea that people trust those whom they already know or with whom the share a personal connection (something that MoveOn and Dean very much utilized). Obama used a total of fifteen social networks (and had five million friends) to direct people to the MyBO Website (Drehle 2008). The following table outlines the Obama Campaign's activity as organized online.

Obama's Facebook page alone had three million supporters, and his Facebook application had 61,000 active users who shared news, blogged, and posted speeches and videos. During the campaign there were more than five hundred Obama groups on Facebook, and one of the first was "Students for Barack Obama." It quickly established chapters at eighty colleges across the country and eventually developed into a structured grassroots movement with a director of field operations, an Internet director, a finance director, and a blog team director (Vargas 2008). Although the group originated on Facebook, it later developed a website of its own with a mailing list and each volunteer team included a data manager, a phone bank coordinator, a campus coordinator, and a volunteer coordinator. Generation Obama (GO) chapters also formed local grassroots groups across the nation that were run and maintained by supporters who held fundraising events, organized volunteers, conducted voter registration drives, and helped turn out the vote (Organizing for America 2007).

Table 5.3 Obama Campaign Activity

E-mail	13 million people on the e-mail list received 7,000 variation of more than 1 billion e-mails
Donors	3 million online donors contributed 6.5 million times
Social Networks	5 million "friends" on more than 15 social networking sites; 3 million friends on Facebook alone
Web Site	8.5 million monthly visitors to MyBarackObama.com (at peak); 2 million profiles with 400,000 blog posts; 35,000 volunteer groups that held 200,000 offline events; 70,000 fundraising hubs that raised $30 million
Video	Nearly 2,000 official YouTube videos; watched more than 80 million times, with 135,000 subscribers; 442,000 user-generated videos on YouTube
Mobile	3 million people signed up for the text messaging program; each received 5 to 20 messages per month
Phone Calls	3 million personal phone calls placed in the last four days of the campaign

Source: Edelman 2009

The goal of the Obama campaign in terms of accessing social networking sites was to lead supporters to MyBO. On the official Obama website the campaign channeled people to the specific activities and causes that were deemed most important to fulfilling the campaign's electoral strategy (Lutz 2008). MyBO maximized group collaboration and gave individual volunteers tasks they could follow on their own schedule with the goal being to "provide opportunities for the most casual supporters to stay involved, while also providing more strenuous opportunities for the smaller core of activists" (Liasson 2008). By the end of the campaign there were two million active users of MyBO, 35,000 affinity groups for Obama, and thirteen million people on his e-mail list (Ambinder 2008). Ultimately, MyBO served as an online platform that offered a campaign blog, detailed supporter profiles, personalized fundraising pages, applications to manage affinity groups, videos, speeches, photos, how-to-guides that gave people materials to create their own content, and event-planning tools. The campaign also deployed a host of social-psychological mechanisms to motivate new forms of electoral participation. For example, on MyBO, participation allowed supporters to earn reputation points that visibly displayed their involvement. It also awarded users points for different activities, thereby creating competition among supporters (Stelter 2008).

MyBO and Obama's profile pages on other social networking sites were used not only as ways to connect volunteers with one another, but also to encourage them to translate their online activism into physical activism in their local areas (as exemplified by student groups earlier). It employed peer-to-peer networking when Hillary Clinton dropped from the race in June of 2008 by activating the e-mail list to ask supporters to rally her supporters by hosting "Unite for Change" house parties in their neighborhoods. Approximately 4,000 parties were held that combined new and old Obama supporters (Stelter 2008). Through the Obama Organizing Fellows initiatives supporters could apply online to volunteer to spend six weeks over the summer to train, and then return to their communities to organize get-out-the-vote drives in conjunction with other on-the-ground fieldwork operations. The "My Neighborhood" button on MyBO allowed visitors to see people and events in their immediate vicinity and "Grassroots Match," a gift-matching program, brought together new donors and their matching donors personally to communicate and reinforce one another's commitment to the campaign (Ambinder 2008).

The unprecedented scope and scale of data collection, which combined generated data with national voter databases amassed from public and commercial sources, was another hallmark of the Obama strategy. Campaign volunteers updated the overall voter outreach database by recording the results from block-walking and other forms of face-to-face grassroots organizing, and this complemented polling data (Delany 2009). Both of these provided information about the effectiveness of canvassing efforts on the ground. MyBO tracked online activities as well, systematically gathering data on how supporters used the applications on the website to capture the results of volunteers' efforts to engage other potential supporters through its online "Neighbor to Neighbor" tool. This also pulled in user data from social networking sites. Additionally, volunteer phone-bankers provided data that the capmpaign used to make strategic decisions about resource allocation (Ambinder 2008). On Election Day the outreach and data-collection operation morphed into a voter-turnout operation as e-mails provided people with the names of five others who supported Obama and asked them to call each one to ensure they were going to the polls, and offer a ride if needed (Dreier 2009). Thus, this peer-to-peer recruitment and mobilization was not activated only in the virtual world but in the material world as well.

In sum, the Obama campaign was heralded as an unparalleled election because of its grassroots, democratic, collaborative, and transparent efforts. It seemingly bypassed the "professional model" by relying on volunteers to recruit, gather and record data, and mobilize supporters online and offline. However, a closer examination of the campaign strategy paints a different picture that will be explored in the following section.

The Not So Bottom-up Approach of the Obama Campaign

Behind the strategizing of the Obama campaign was a digital consulting firm called Blue State Digital (BSD). It purchased the services of BSD to manage the online fundraising, constituency-building, issue advocacy, and the peer-to-peer networking and community-building aspects of the campaign. Rospars and other former Dean aides formed BSD in 2004 in an attempt to refine the Internet techniques pioneered by Dean (Hindman 2005). By 2005 it had developed the ability to track features that supported the logging of detailed supporter profiles and the narrowcasting of political communications. It also was able to integrate the activities of design and branding, web and video content, mass e-mail and text messaging, and online advertising, organizing, and fundraising. On its website it states: "For every constituent in your list, our constituent viewer allows you to see an individual's contributions, email actions (opens, click-through, and forwards), signup information, initiations sent to a friend, petitions signed, and every other action they have taken through your site. With this picture, you can target emails to in individuals or groups who meet particular profiles (for example, likely repeat donors, or avid email forwarders)" (bluestatedigital.com).

With the assistance of BSD the Obama team developed more than 7,000 customized e-mails to individual prospects (over two billion landed in inboxes), which were continually and extensively subject to testing and refinement, from sender's names to subject lines, topics, text, imagery, and link placement (Delany 2009). Campaign staff broke their supporter list into several randomized groups, whose members would then receive different e-mails based on the message or feature being tested. Once they analyzed the results (messages opened, actions taken, donations made, etc.) and cross-referenced this with the list demographics, staff applied this information to the next round of e-mail, which in turn yielded more testing data, which yielded more messages, which yielded more data, etc. (Sternberg 2008, E4). Hence, supporters received messages with different content based on their state or congressional district, their interests, their demographics, donations, or their past pattern of actions on behalf of the campaign. E-mails were segmented according to the demographic information citizens gave the campaign, the actions they had taken, and other involvement on campaign platforms. Rosbar described MyBO's use of its e-mail list in the following way: "The point is not to have a million people sign up. The point is to be able to chop up that million-person list into manageable chunks and organize them" (Stelter 2008).

The Obama analytic team, in conjunction with the services of BSD, also solicited different amounts of money based on a person's donation history, and tailored e-mails accordingly. It practiced a similar tactic with its advertisements on the Web. Throughout the campaign political ads were delivered online based on cookies that tracked browsing habits or relational data collected on social networking sites (Delany 2009). The media team spent $16 million to buy ad space on Facebook, for example, and the Obama staff tracked which ad at what time drew the most traffic, and then would respond with follow up ads (Stelter 2008). In essence, what BSD does is reminiscent of McGinnis' (1988) and other scholars' description of how candidates hired advertising agencies to sell them to citizens when the central source of information for most of the electorate was television. These agencies have been replaced in large part by digital political consulting firms as they narrowcast political communication premised on personal portraits of citizens assembled through commercial, public, and generated data (Kreiss 2009).

Whereas MyBO provided citizens with the opportunity to create digital social networks of relatives, friends, neighbors, and co-workers—encouraging supporters to attract others to the campaign—this data was then integrated, coordinated and used for further mobilizing efforts. The campaign's use of Facebook Connect (an application that allowed users to synchronize data between Facebook and external sites) for instance, enabled supporters to publicize their activities on MyBO to their wider social networks to help recruit and mobilize additional supporters (Sternberg 2008). These networks, in turn, became the conduits of the campaign's political messages and consequently citizens were not the primary agents of their communicative participation as the campaign was able to directly leverage these external social networks.

THEORIZING NEW DIGITAL TECHNOLOGIES
IN INSTITUTIONALIZED POLITICS

Although this chapter focuses on institutional politics, during the 2008 election there were discussions about whether or not the Obama campaign represented a social movement given its message of "hope," "yes we can," and "change we can believe in." I would contend, however, that it was not really representative of a social movement in that there was never a single, overarching struggle that represented a specific constituency. Yet, very specific aspects of framing and resource mobilization theories can aptly be used to assess the dynamics of Obama's strategy. Through the framing of the message the campaign did successfully persuade a large segment of the population that there were urgent issues that needed to be addressed at a societal/political level, that alternatives were possible, and that supporters and volunteers could be invested with agency. This supports the importance of framing analysis advocated by a number of researchers (Taylor and Van-Dyke 2004; Diani 1996; Benford 1993; Gamson and Wolsfield 1993; Snow and Benford 1988; Snow et al. 1986). Although not organized in a specific way or for a specific cause, the number of young volunteers and their mistrust of institutional, mainstream politics provided Obama with a large segment of the population that could be tapped into. The mobilization of the Obama campaign is also similar to organization style of NSMs in that it was anchored in fluid networks within an opt-in, opt-out dynamic, and that the technology used blurred the private and public spheres. Habermas' (1993, 1989) perspective of NSMs as struggles to reestablish the public sphere and participatory democracy was also evident in the mobilization. It was new ICTs and other media platforms that served as a resource that could most adroitly harness this readiness for change, recruit new members, fundraise, and mobilize.

Thus, theories of ICTs are the most appropriate analytical framework within which to situate the Obama campaign. As noted in the previous chapters, it is well-established that new ICTs can lead to a better informed citizenry and allow for new opportunities for the creation, sharing, and exchange of information as well as new types of activism (Carty 2009; Bennett and Iyengar 2008; Jenkins 2006; Langman 2005; Kellner 2004; Kidd 2003). These "virtual public spheres" of the Internet facilitate what Kahn and Kellner (2003) call "post-subcultures" which are fluid and interpersonal networks of discussion, debate and clarification. These applications were evident during the 2008 election, as were claims among scholars that new ICTs allow for the development of community and face-to-face civic engagement regardless of virtual ties (Bennett et al. 2009; Best and Krueger 2006; Jenkins 2006; Pasek et al. 2006; Nipp 2004; Katz and Rice 2002). They are also indicative of Castell's (2007) conception of a new kind of civil society based on the "electronic grassrooting of democracy" through the many-to-many flow of information across horizontal links. For it was across digital forms of communication that messages were framed and collective identity forged among Obama supporters. The new media platforms, as used by volunteers in the campaign also support the propositions of scholars who view new technologies as enabling exposure to new ideas and allow viewers and senders of information to add their own input within certain parameters (Jenkins 2006; Van Aelst and Walgrave 2003; Diani 2000; Kollock and Smith 1999; Pliskin and Romm 1997).

The electoral process also raises similar questions as the mobilization of MoveOn did in the previous chapter. The "tell a friend" phenomenon and forwarding of e-mails, and the resulting interest of the recipient on the basis of trust of the source questions contentions that people only seek out information relevant to them as proposed by Bimber and Davis (2001) and Bimber (1998) and that online interaction is mainly composed of like-minded people who are often predisposed to issues that Jordan (2001) and Diani (2000) warn about. This case study also illuminates how online organizing and networking often leads to political and civic engagement in "real" communities as web-based ties and social relations often spill over into the material world, and organizers can then mobilize these groups to strengthen advocacy networks. This adds credence to research that finds community-based activism closely related to, or initiated by online activism and organizing (Jenkins 2006; Nipp 2004; Bennett 2003).

The 2008 presidential campaign challenges many of the optimistic theories that emphasize the on-hierarchical nature of online interaction and view ICTs and facilitating participatory democracy (see Garrett 2006; Hampton 2003; McCaughney and Ayers 2000; Arquilla and Ronfledt 2001; Brainard and Siplon 2000; Wellman 2000). More specifically, Bimber's (2003) view of the democratizing process of collective and political action, based on collaborative decision-making and self-governing styles of organization is questionable given the role of BSD and Obama's media team.

The election highlighted the symbiotic relationship between new and old media and illustrated that there may be more continuity between the two rather than a full blown "technological revolution" that has replaced conventional forms of mass media. Challenging the celebratory perspectives of the digital revolution, a more thorough understanding of the social and political implications of new ICTs on social change reveals elite domination and control over aspects of cyberspace, as well as the fact that professional managers can extend their power and control through new media platforms (Hindman 2007; Lievouw and Livingston 2006; Dimaggio et al. 2004). The way the campaign operated demonstrated that public opinion, despite new forms of technology is still administered by political elites at least to a certain degree through the mediation of public opinion. To revisit Habermas' fears about the impact of the mass media on public opinion, this analysis highlights that it is still manufactured by media experts, polls, and political consulting agencies as they shape, construct and limit public discourse around topics relevant to, and validated and approved by operators of ICTs (it merely occurs within a new communicative system). Although topics of common interest and political issues were being discussed among Obama supporters, ultimately the Obama staffers and BSD controlled what was being discussed and who was receiving what kind of information.

Howard's (2006) work is useful in theorizing the Obama' team's undemocratic use of technology. He argues that linkages that are created through digital tools, designed to create networks of connections from past e-mail communications and Internet use, can be manipulated by elites who select citizens as receptors of political communication without the knowledge of the real person based on their "data shadows." Through various registration requirements and the gathering and selling of demographic and psychographic information they create databases of voter profiles and consequently citizens can be marketed through the control of ICTs via intermediaries. Additionally, lobbyists, politicians, and interest groups often argue on behalf of profiles without the explicit support of the real person casting the shadow. His depiction of how the e-politics community rests to a large degree upon the practices of data mining, political redlining, and narrowcasting can be applied to the mechanisms of Obama's media team and, use their of the Internet and MyBO specifically. He highlights that, based upon the information gathered through data mining, and much the information collected without informed consent, certain types of information are then kept from some citizens, whereas others are presented freely and frequently. Thus, although the Internet contains a vast amount of information not available in the past, users may not always have access to it due to redlining.

Through the use of narrowcasting the Obama team accessed data sets assembled from computer-cookies to send direct messages to people who visited the websites. It maximized the reach of messages by capitalizing on social intimacy as supporters urged their network ties to support his candidacy, thus turning citizens into political advertisers. In exchange for their support, they were marketed and monitored at an unprecedented rate, while at the same time seemingly acting as independent agents. This demonstrates that despite the emergence of multiple axes of information do indeed provide new opportunities for citizens to challenge elite control of politics, these are in many ways still shaped by structures of power. Despite grassroots efforts, political elites are still very much a part of the political campaign process as new computerized forms of communication are used to create "managed citizens"—meaning that political managers are using digital media not merely to collect public opinion, but also to create it. Howard elaborates, "We now have the power to have our interests represented without behaving as a traditional citizenry" (p. 187).

Although interaction has greatly increased due to the Internet, citizens were not included in more substantive forms of participation in the online world as e-mails often serve as one-way flows of communication (this was alluded to in the last chapter regarding MoveOn). Recipients can reply to e-mails and action alerts, but don't receive responses, and there are no institutionalized forums for debate on meaningful matters of policy. For example, to protest Obama's support to renew the FISA (Foreign Intelligence Surveillance Act) legislation, which offered retroactive immunity for the telecommunications firms that assisted the Bush administration in its wiretapping program, activists created the MyBO group, Get FISA Right in July of 2008. This was the largest self-organized group on MyBO, consisting of over 18,000 members (Ruffini 2008). Obama responded through a written statement on his website explaining his position but there was no actual dialogue between him and concerned supporters that challenged his perspective. Therefore, whereas MoveOn and the Obama campaign made inroads into peer-to-peer networking and more democratic forms of communication in some specific ways, the Internet has not yet been used as a medium to genuinely listen to or respond to its supporters as a group.

To conclude, although the stated qualities of "openness, transparency, and participation" of the Obama campaign seem to merge well with the Internet, the integration of mobilization and recruitment efforts by professional management was accomplished through a system coordinated and monitored by the Obama team. It perfected ways of taking advantage of commercial sites such as Facebook, MySpace, and YouTube that served as mediums for marketing, communications, and fundraising, especially among younger citizens. To be sure, volunteer organizing and mobilizing was far less bureaucratic than in previous elections, and played a huge role in Obama's successful presidential bid, but these were ultimately controlled through a top-down structure and hierarchical forms of communication. Although citizen agency to share information, organize, recruit, fundraise, and participate in canvassing efforts was clearly enhanced to a certain extent through social networking sites and new Internet tools, these operated within a context of structured interactivity and ultimately, elite control. The Obama staff systematically, through sophisticated measures, aggregated and analyzed data through professional consultants, who then tapped into peer-to-peer networks on social networking and other sites for the institutional ends of the campaign, i.e. fundraising, voter identification, and mobilization. What this chapter suggests is that much more research is needed to assess the potential undemocratic nature of the technological revolution and tries to expand on the limited dialogue that currently exists.

Conclusion

This book has set out to advance the theorization of collective behavior across the domains of contentious and electoral politics. I chose four diverse case studies to examine, empirically and conceptually, the various dynamics and characteristics of each within an overarching theoretical framework which brings together various models that have been employed in past previous research. I have not attempted to reinvent the wheel, but rather make theoretical connections between analytical frameworks within the current literature to offer a more comprehensive model that does not privilege one paradigm over another. In doing so I strove to illuminate the overlapping concepts and theories used in political science, sociology, and communication studies to yield a more unified framework that can be generalized across the various disciplines. This can perhaps broaden the focus of social movement research and increase the applicability to other forms of collective behavior while also avoiding the often fragmented and partial perspectives as applied to case studies.

In the previous four chapters, each analysis addressed the conditions for the emergence of collective behavior, the context within which it formed and sustained itself, recruitment efforts among participants, mobilization dynamics, and consequences of collective behavior. I acknowledge in each case study that there is a political, socio-historical, and cultural context to which groups and individuals respond, as well as macro-, meso-, and micro-level dynamics in which they are situated. The variety of theories that I use to examine each case study explains both the how (the more descriptive side of social movements) and the why (the theoretical explanatory dimension). This comprehensive analytical framework posits that neither cultural theories, resource mobilization, nor structural theories on their own can sufficiently explain social movement phenomena, but demonstrates ways in which they are interconnected in complex ways. Each contextualizes how actors took advantage of existing political opportunities, forged alliances and coalitions that expanded their support base, and expressed their goals through framing to recruit new participants.

In addition to advancing a more unified theoretical model that can be used for future social movement research, another contribution that this book makes is to refine our understanding of how new technologies are affecting contentious politics, civil society processes, and institutional politics. Historically, the control over outlets of communication and information has been a key source of power and counter-power across political and social boundaries. This control has furthered the agendas of powerful groups at times, and marginalized groups at others. With new ICTs and forms of digital media social actors can mobilize quickly and cheaply on both a local and global level across virtual and material spheres of social life.

In many instances it was the Internet, alternative media, and other forms of advanced communication systems that facilitated the struggle of social movement actors in terms of organizing protests, information-sharing, establishing collective identity and building solidarity, and offering counter views of the status quo. E-activism and e-mobilizations have allowed for new forms of grassroots participatory democracy that often bypass mainstream and corporate political and media, and demonstrate the symbiotic relationship between e-activism and local organizing as online and offline activism tend to reinforce each with groups straddling cyberspace and local mobilizations. This calls for new theoretical examination and a reconceptualization of concepts such as mobilization, collective identity, and participatory democracy that were traditionally formulated to encompass face-to-face contacts, and this holds true for both contentious and institutional politics.

However, this research also warns against the idealization of the technological revolution and calls for recognition of the continuity between old and new forms of communication, and the ability of elites to manipulate and control the new communication environment. As the last chapter argued (and Chapter 4 to a lesser extent), despite new media platforms and other technologies that allow for horizontal flows of information and peer-to-peer networking, powerful groups still have ways of controlling these new communication venues. New digital media and social networking sites have not necessarily shifted the balance of power away from the profession model and toward grassroots empowerment, and this complex combination of new digital media/technologies and old gate keepers needs to be theoretically assessed through a more critical gaze.

In sum, I intend this book to provide a conceptual and theoretical trajectory that can be used as a springboard for further examination of disruptive and institutional politics. One compelling question for future research on social movements is how to categorize and theorize online groups like MoveOn that are part virtual and part concrete. Chapter 4 merely scratches the surface, but to what extent such organizations are being replicated, and for what causes, opens up new areas of research. These groups also muddy the waters in trying to distinguish between interest groups, dissident groups, and SMOs. The emergence of similar mobilizations that represent something of a hybrid are typical of what some scholars refer to as "social movement communities" rather than social movements per se, which is another fruitful area of research that needs to be investigated in more detail.

References

48 hours. 1996. Program aired October 17.

Adbusters. Available at http://www.adbusters.org. Accessed 2/2/03.

Agence France Presse. 2004. "Tens of Thousands Throng to London to Protest Iraq War." October 17, p. 22.

Aguera, Martin. 2003. "Collateral Damage?" *Defense News*, February 17, pp. 1–8.

Alternet.org. Available at http://www.alternet.org. Accessed 10/10/06.

Ambinder, Marc. 2008. "How To Tell Your VoteBuilders From Your MyBOs, Your Catalysts From Your VANs." *The Atlantic*, November 14. Available at http://marcambinder.theatlantic.com/archives/2008/11/technology_catalist_votebuilde.php. Accessed 5/5/09.

Amenta, Edwin and Michael P. Young. 1999. "Making an Impact: The Conceptual and Methodological Implications of the Collective Benefits Criterion." pp. 22–41 in *How Social Movements Matter*, edited by M. Giugni, D. McAdam and C. Tilly. Minneapolis, MN: University of Minnesota Press.

———, and Neal Caren. 2004. "The Legislative, Organizational, and Beneficiary Consequences of State-Oriented Challenges." pp. 461–488 in *The Blackwell Companion to Social Movements*, edited by David Snow, Sarah Soule and Hanspeter Kriesi. Malden, MA and Oxford, UK: Blackwell Publishing.

———, and Neal Caren and Edwin Loasky. 2005. "Age for Leisure? Political Mediation and the Impact of the Pension Movement on U.S. Old-Age Policy." *American Sociological Review* 70(3): 516–538.

Andrews, Kenneth. 2001. "Social Movements and Policy Implementation: The Mississippi Civil Rights Movement and the War on Poverty, 1965–1971." *American Sociological Review* 59: 678–702.

Armstrong, Jerome and Markos Zúniga. 2006. *Netroots, Grassroots, and the Rise of People-Powered Politics*. White River Junction, VT: Chelsea Green Publishing Company.

Arquilla, John and David Ronfeldt. 1996. *The Zapatista Social Network War in Mexico*. RAND: Washington, DC.

———. 2001. *Networks and Netwars: The Future of Terror*. Santa Monica, CA: Rand Corporation.

———. Arsenault, Amelia and Manuel Casttels. 2006. "Conquering the Minds, Conquering Iraq." *Information, Communication & Society* 9(3): 284–307.

Aun, Fred. 2007. "MySpace Digs Deeper Into Politics With Town Hall Meetings." *E-Commerce Times*. Available at http://www.ecommercetimes.com/story/57327.html. Accessed 4/9/08.

Backman, Rachel and Brent Hunsberger. 2008. "Phil Knight's Influence Transforms University of Oregon Athletics." *Oregonian*, May 4, p. D1.

Bacon, David. 2004. "The Children of NAFTA. Labor Wars on the U.S./Mexican Border." Univeristy of California Press: Berkley and Los Angeles.

Bandy, Joe and Jennifer Bickham Mendez. 2003. "A Place of Their Own? Women Organizers in the Maquilas of Nicaragua and Mexico." *Mobilization: An International Quarterly* 8(22): 173–188.

Baudrillard, Jean. 1988. *Jean Baudrillard: Selected Writings*. Stanford, CA: Stanford University Press.

Baum, Bob. 1996. "Jordan won't Speak for Nike on Use of Child Labor." *Oregonian*, July 16, p. D2.

Bauman, Zygmunt. 1997. *Postmodernity and its Discontents*. New York, NY: NYU Press.

BBC Online. 2004. "Iraq War Illegal, says Annan." Available at http://news.bbc.co.uk/1/hi/world/middle_east/3661134.stm. Accessed 10/24/05.

Beck, Ulrich. 2006. *Cosmopolitan Vision*. Cambridge, MA: Polity Press.

Benford, Robert. 1993. "Frame Disputes within the Nuclear Disarmament Movement." *Social Forces* 71(3): 677–702.

———, and David Snow. 2000. "Framing Processes and Social Movements: An Overview and Assessment." *Annual Review of Sociology* 26: 611–639.

———, and Scott Hunt. 1988. "Dramaturgy and Social Movements: The Social Construction and Communication of power." *Sociological Inquiry* 62: 36–55.

Bennet, Daniel and Pam Fielding. 1999. *The Net Effect: How Cyber-Advocacy is Changing the Political Landscape*. Washington: Capitol Advantage.

Bennett, Sue, Karl Maton and Lisa Dervin. 2009. "The 'Digital Natives' Debate: A Critical Review of the Evidence." *British Journal of Educational Technology* 34(5): 775–786.

Bennett, William. 2003. "Communicating Global Activism." *Information, Communication and Society* 6(2): 143–168.

———, and Shanto Iyengar. 2008. "A New Era of Minimal Effects? The Changing Foundations of Political Communication." *Journal of Communication* 58(4): 707–731.

Bennis, Phyllis. 2003. "Going Global: Building a Movement against Empire." *ZNet*. Available at http://www.zcomminucations.org/going-global-building-a-movement-against-empire-by-phyllis-bennis. Accessed 5/29/03.

Berman, Ari. 2007. "Not Your Father's Antiwar Activist." *The Nation*, pp. 32–37.

Best, Samuel and Brian Krueger. 2006. "Online Interaction and Social Capitals." *Social Science Computer Review* 24(4): 305–410.

Best, Steven and Douglas Kellner. 1991. *Postmodern Theory: Critical Interrogations*. New York, NY: Guilford Press.

———. 1997. *The Post-modern Turn*. New York, NY: Guilford Press.

Bimber, Bruce. 1998. "The Internet and Political Transformation: Populism, Community and Accelerated Pluralism." *Polity* 31(1): 133–160.

———. 2003. *Information and American Democracy: Technology in the Evolution of Political Power*. Cambridge, MA: Cambridge University Press.

———, and Richard Davis. *Campaigning Online: The Internet and U.S. Elections*. New York, NY: Oxford University Press.

Blue State Digital. Available at http://www.bluestatedigital.com. Accessed 9/14/09.

Blumer, Herbert. 1939. *Critiques of research in the social sciences: An appraisal of Thomas and Znaniecki's The Polish peasant in Europe and America*. New York, NY: Social Science Research Council.

Bowley, Graham. 2004. "Anger Against Blair over Iraq War." *Herald Tribune*, June 12, p. B6.

Boyd, Andrew. 2003. "The Web Rewires the Movement." *The Nation*. Available at http://www.thenation.com/doc/20030804/boyd. Accessed 3/30/04.

Brainard, Lori and Patricia Siplon. 2000. "Cyberspace Challenges to Nonprofit Organizations." *Administration and Society* 34(2): 141–175.

Brecher, Jeremy, Tim Costello and Brendan Smith. 2000. *Globalization From Below: The Power of Solidarity*. Cambridge, MA: South End Press.

Briggs, Paul. 1996. "Union-Backed Group Protest against Nike's Presence." *University of Maryland Publications*, November 18, p. 7.

Brownstein, Ronald. 2004. "MoveOn Works the Hollywood Spotlight to Amplify Its Voice." *Los Angeles Times,* July 4, p. B7.

Buechler, Steven M. 1993. "Beyond Resource Mobilization? Emerging Trends in Social Movement Theory." *The Sociological Quarterly* 34(2): 217–235.

———. 1999. *Social Movements in Advanced Capitalism: The Political Economy and Cultural Construction of Social Activism*. New York, NY: Oxford University Press.

Bulman, Robin. 1996. "Nike's Tainted Cash." *Journal of Commerce*, July 23, p. 6.

Burress, Charles. 2003. "Making Their Move." *San Francisco Chronicle*, February 9, p. A23.

Burstein, Paul. 1998. "Bringing the Public Back In: Should Sociologists Consider the Impact of Public Opinion on Public Policy?" *Social Forces* 77: 27–62.

———, and April Linton. 2002. "The Impact of Political Parties, Interest Groups, and Social Movement Organizations on Public Policy: Some Recent Evidence and Theoretical Concerns." *Social Forces* 81(2): 381–408.

Callinicos, Alex. 2005. "Anti-war Protests Do Make a Difference." *Socialist Worker*. Available at http://www.socialistworker.co.uk/art.php?id=6067.Accessed 3/30/2005.

Campaign for Labor Rights. Available at http://www.clr@igc.org. Accessed 1/4/02.

Canizares, Kristina. 2001. "Nike's Corporate Responsibility Sham." Available at http://www.alternet.org/story/10931/nike%27_corporate_responsibility_sham. Accessed 4/10/02.

Carty, Victoria. 2005. "Textual Portrayals of Female Athletes: Liberation Or Nuanced Forms of Patriarchy?" *Frontiers: A Journal of Women's Studies* 26(2): 132–172.

———. 2009. "The Anti-War Movement versus the War against Iraq." *International Journal of Peace Studies*. 14(1): 17–38.

———. 2009. "SMOs, Cyberactivism and Entertainment as Politics: How MoveOn is Expanding Public Discourse and Political Struggle." pp. 58–81 in *Engaging Social Justice: Critical Studies of the Twenty-first Century Social Transformations*, edited by David Fasenfest. Boston: Brill Publishers.

———. 2010. "Bridging Contentious and Electoral Politics: MoveOn and the Digital Revolution." *Research in Social Movements, Conflict and Change*. Volume 30, forthcoming.

Castells, Manuel. 1989. *The Informational City: Information Technology, Economic Restructuring and the Urban Regional Process*. Oxford, UK, Malden, MA: Blackwell Press.

———. 1997. *The Power of Identity (The Information Age: Economy, Society and Culture, Volume II)*. Oxford, UK: Blackwell Press.

———. 2001. The Internet Galaxy: Reflections on the Internet, Business and Society. Malden, MA: Blackwell Publishers.

———. 2007. "Communication, Power and Counter-power in the Network Society." *International Journal of Communication* 1: 238–266.

Cave, Michael. 2002. "Just Change It." *Australian Financial Review*, June 14, p. 12.

cbsnews.com. Available at http://www.cbsnews.com/stories/2003101/23/opinions/polls/man5377739s.html. Accessed 10/1/04.

Center for Information and Research on Civic Learning and Engagement. 2008. "Young Voters in the 2008 Presidential Election." Available athttp://www.civicyouth.org/PopUps/FactSheets/FS_08_exit_polls.pdf. Accessed 8/28/09.

Center for Responsive Politics. 2008. "Moveon.org Independent Expenditures." Available at http://www.opensecrets.org/pacs/indexpend. php?cycle=2008&cmte=C00341396. Accessed 4/7/09.

Chaudry, Lakshmi. 2004. "A Soldier Speaks: Robert Sarra." *Alternet.org.* Available at http://www.alternet.org/asoldierspeaks/20337. Accessed 11/13/04.

Cleaver, Harry. 1998. "The Zapatista Effect: The Internet and Rise of an Alternative Fabric." *Journal of International Affairs* 51(2): 621–640.

cnn.com. "Democrats Follow at a Dividing Day at the UN." Available at http://www.cnn.com/2003/US/0215/sprj.irg.protests. Accessed 11/9/04.

Cohen, Jean L. 1983. "Rethinking Social Movements." *Berkeley Journal of Sociology* 28: 97–113.

———. 1985. Strategy and Identity: New Theoretical Paradigms and Contemporary Social Movements. *Social Research* 52: 663–716.

Cowell, Alan. 2007. "London Bomb Plot Trial Begins." *International Herald Tribune*, January 15, p. 11.

Coy, Patrick, Lynne Woehrle and Gregory Maney. 2005. "Harnessing and Challenging U.S. Hegemony: The U.S. Peace Movement after 9/11." *Sociological Perspectives* 38: 357–381.

Deans, Jason. 2004. "Fox News Documentary Tops Amazon Sales Chart." *Guardian Unlimited News.* Available at http://www.film.gaurdian.co.uk/news/story/012589/html. Accessed 8/1/04.

Delany, Colin. 2009. "Learning from Obama: Lessons for Online Communication in 2009 and Beyond." *E-Politics*, August. Available at http://www.epolitics.com/learning-from-obama.pdf. Accessed 6/10/09.

Diamond, Larry and Richard Gunther. 2001. *Political Parties and Democracy.* Baltimore, MD: Johns Hopkins University Press.

Diani, Mario. 2000. "Social Movement Networks Virtual and Real." *Information, Communication and Society* 3(3): 386–401.

———, and Doug McAdam. 2003. *Social Movements and Networks, Relational Approaches to Collective Action.* New York, NY: Oxford University Press

Dicken, Peter. 1998. *Global Shift.* 3rd edition. New York, NY: Guilford Press.

Dimaggio, Paul, Hargitta Eszter, Russell Neuman and John Robinson. 2004. "Social Implications of the Internet." *American Sociological Review* 27: 307–332.

Dobnik, Verence. 1997. "Activist Finds Abuses at Vietnam Nike Plants." *Washington Post*, March 28, p. G2.

Dodson, Sean and Ben Hammersley. 2003. "The Web's Candidate for President." *The Guardian.* Available at http://www.gaurdian.co.uk/media/2003/dec/18/newmedia.uselections2004. Accessed 4/19/07.

Drehle, David Von. 2008. "Obama's Youth Vote Triumph." *Time Magazine*, January 4, pp. 15–17.

Dreier, Peter. 2009. "Organizing in the Obama Years: A Progressive Moment or a New Progressive Era?" *COMM-ORG: The On-Line Conference on Community Organizing and Development.* Available at http://comm-org.wisc.edu/papers2009/dreier.htm#ntroduction. Accessed 10/10/09.

———, and Richard Applebaum. 2003. "Foot Fault." *The American Prospect,* September/October, pp. 24–31.

Drenttel, William. 2007. "MoveOn's Muddled Symbolism." *The New Republic*, June 28, p.17.

Dür, Andreas. 2008. "Bargaining Power and Trade Liberalization: European External Trade Policies in the 1960s." European Journal of International Relations, 14: 645–669.

Dutta-Bergman, M. J. 2006. "Community Participation and Internet Use After September 11: Complementarily in Channel Consumption." Journal of Computer-Mediated Communication, 11(2). Available at http://jcmc.indiana.edu/vol11.issue2dutta-bergman.html. Accessed 4/1/08.

Dwyer, Jim. 1996. "Those Sneakers Really Stink." *Daily News*, July 18, p. 3.

Earl, Jennifer. 2004. "The Cultural Consequences of Social Movements." pp. 508–530 in *The Blackwell Companion to Social Movements*, edited by David Snow, Sarah Soule and Hanspeter Kriesi. Malden, MA and Oxford, UK, Blackwell Publishing.

———, and Alan Schussman. 2003. "The New Site of Activism: Online Organizations, Movement Entrepreneurs the Changing Location of Social Movement Decision Making." *Research in Social Movements and Change* 24: 155–87.

Edelman 2009. "The Social Pulpit: Barack Obama's Social Media Toolkit." Available at http://edelman.com. Accessed 10/14/09.

Egan, Timothy. 1998. "The Swoon of the Swoosh." *New York Times Magazine*, September 13, pp. 66–70.

Elliot, Andrea. 2007. "Where Boys Grow up to Be Jihadis." *New York Times Magazine*, November 25, pp. 69–74, 98–100.

Evans, Peter. 2000. "Fighting Marginalization with Transnational Networks: Counter-hegemonic Globalization." *Contemporary Sociology* 29: 230–241.

Farrell, Stephen. 2008. "US Combat Troops would leave by 2011 Under Draft Agreement." *Herald Tribune*, August 22, p. 21.

Featherstone, Liza. 2002. *Students Against Sweatshops*. New York, NY: Verso.

Federal Elections Commission. 2006. Available at http://www.fec-gov/disclosure.shtml. Accessed 10/10/09.

Franklin, Jonathan and Paul Harris. 2003. "An Unprecedented Internet Campaign Waged on the Frontline and in the US is Exposing the Real Risks for the Troops in Iraq." *The Guardian*, June 9, pp. 24–27.

Frey, R. Scott, Thomas Dietz and Linda Kalof. 1991. "On the Utility of Robust and Resampling Strategies." *Rural Sociology* 56: 461–474.

Fullilove, Michael. 2007. "Ally with Attitude." *New York Times*, November 29, p. A23.

Future Majority. 2008. "Youth Vote (Ages 18–29) Support in Presidential Elections." Available at http://www.futuremajority.com/. Accessed 10/11/09.

Gamson, William. 1975. *The Strategy of Social Protest*. Homewood, IL: Dorsey Press.

———. 1990. *The Strategy of Social Protest*. Belmont, CA: Wadsworth.

———. 1992. *Talking Politics*. New York, NY: Cambridge University Press.

———, and David Meyer. 1996. *Comparative Perspectives on Social Movements*. Cambridge, MA: Cambridge University Press.

———, and David Meyer. 1996. "Framing Political Opportunity." pp. 275–290 in *Comparative Perspectives on Social Movements: Political Opportunities, Mobilizing Structures, and Framing*, edited by Doug McAdam, John McCarthy and Meyer Zald. New York, NY/Cambridge, MA: Cambridge University Press.

Ganz, Marshall. 2004. "Organizing as Leadership." In *Encyclopedia of Leadership*, edited by George Goethals, Georgia J. Sorenson, James McGregor Burns. Thousand Oaks, CA: Sage Publications, pp. 1134–1144.

Garrett, R. Kelly. 2006. Protest in an Information Society: A Review of Literature on Social Movements and New ICTs. *Information, Communication & Society* (9)2: 202–224.

Gereffi, Gary and Miguel Korzeniewicz. 1990. "Commodity Chains and Footwear Exports in the Semiperiphery." pp. 145–168 in *Semiperipheral States in the World-Economy*, edited by William Martin. Westport, CT: Greenwood Press.

Giddens, Anthony. 1991. *Modernity and Self-Identity. Self and Society in the Late Modern Age*. Cambridge, MA: Polity.

Giugni, Marco. 1998. "Was it worth the effort? The Outcomes and Consequences of Social Movements." *Annual Review of Sociology* 98: 371–393.

———, and Doug McAdam and Charles Tilly. 1999. *How Social Movements Matter*. Minneapolis, MN: University of Minnesota Press.

Gitlin, Todd. 2005. "America's Age of Empire: The Bush Doctrine." *Mother Jones*. Available at http://www.motherjones.com. Accessed 10/4/06.

Global Exchange. Available at http://globalexchange.org. Accessed 1/7/02.

Goldberg, Jonah. 2008. "Idle Youth Vote." *National Review*. Available at. http://findarticles.com/p/articles/mi_m1282/is_16_60/ai_n28028537. Accessed 2/5/09.

Goldberg, Michelle. 2002. "The Antiwar Movement Goes Mainstream." *Salon.com*. Available at www.salon.com/politics/feature/2002/12/12/peace/index_np.htm. Accessed 5/11/04.

Goldstone, Jack. 2003. *States, Political Parties and Social Movements*. Cambridge, MA: Cambridge University Press.

Goodwin, Jeff, Jasper, James and Francesca Polletta. 2001. *Passionate Politics: Emotions and Social Movements*. Chicago, IL: University of Chicago Press.

Greenhouse, Steven. 1999. "Duke to Adopt a Code to Prevent Apparel from Being Made in Sweatshops." *New York Times*, December 19, p. A8.

———. 1999. "Student Critics Push Attacks on an Association Meant to Prevent Sweatshops." *New York Times*, April 25, p. A18.

Guest, Avery and Susan Wierzbicki. 1999. "Social Ties at the Neighborhood Level." *Urban Affairs Review* 35(1): 92–111.

Gusfield, Joseph. 1962. "Mass Society and Extremist Politics." *American Sociological Review* 27: 19–30.

———. 1970. *Protest, Reform, and Revolt; a Reader in Social Movements*. New York, NY: Wiley.

———. 1994. "The Reflexivity of Social Movements: Collective Behavior and Mass Society Theory Revisited." pp. 58–78 in *New Social Movements. From Ideology to Identity*, edited by E. Laraña, Hank Johnston and J. Gusfield. Philadelphia, PA: Temple University Press.

Habermas, Jurgen. 1981. *The Theory of Communicative Action*. London, UK: Beacon Press.

———. 1983. *Moral Consciousness and Communicative Action*. Cambridge, MA: MIT Press.

———. 1984. *The Theory of Communicative Action*, Volume 1, *Reason and the Rationalization of Society*. Boston, MA: Beacon Press.

———. 1989. *The Structural Transformation of the Public Sphere*. Cambridge, MA: MIT Press.

———. 1993. *Justification and Application: Remarks on Discourse Ethics*. Polity Press, Cambridge.

Hanh, Thich Nhat. 1987. *Interbeing: Fourteen Guidelines for Engaged Buddhism*. Berkeley, CA: Parallax Press.

Hampton, Keith. 2003. "Grieving for a Lost Network: Collective Activism in a Wired Suburb." *The Information Society* 19(5): 417–428.

Haraway, Dana. 1991. *Simians, Cyborgs, and Women*. New York, NY: Routledge Press.

Harris, John and Peter McKay. 1996. "Companies Agree to Meet on Sweatshops." *Washington Post*, August 8, p. A10.

Harris, Scott. 2003. "Anti-war Movement Marshals Forces." *San Jose Mercury*, February 3, 2003, p. A8.

Harvey, David. 1989. *The Condition of Postmodernity: An Inquiry into the Origins of Social Change*. Durham, NC: Duke University Press.

Harvey, N. 1998. *The Chiapas Rebellion: The Struggle for Land and Democracy*. Durham, NC: Duke University Press.

Healy, Patrick. 2006. "Lamont Defeats Lieberman in Primary." *The New York Times*. Available at http://www.nytimes.com/2006/08/08/nyregion/08cnd-campaign.html. Accessed 4/17/07.

Heaney, Michael and Fabio Rojas. 2007. "Partisans, Nonpartisans, and the Antiwar Movement in the United States." *American Politics Research* 35:431464.

Heffernan, Virginia. 2008. "Clicking and Choosing." *The New York Times*, November 1, p. A13.

Herbert, Bob. 1996. "Nike's Pyramid Scheme." *The New York Times*, June 10, p. A12.

Hesseldahl, Arik, Douglas McMillan and Olga Kharif. 2008. "The Vote: A Victory for Social Media, Too." *BusinessWeek*, November 5, p. 15.

Hickey, Roger. 2004. "Onward Deaniacs." *Wireless Innovator*, March 18. Available at http://wirelessinnovator.com/index.php?articleID=2873&sectionID=4. Accessed 4/19/07.

hindustantimes.com. Available at http://www.hindustantimes.com/news/181_1448119,001301780003.htm. Accessed 9/1/05.

Hindman, Matthew. 2005. "The Real Lessons on Howard Dean: Reflections on the First Digital Campaign." *Perspectives on Politics* 3(1): 121–128.

———. 2007. "Open-source Politics Reconsidered: Emerging Patterns in Online Political Participation." pp. 143–170 in *Governance and Information Technology: From Electronic Government to Information Government*, edited by Viktor Mayer-Schonberger and David Lazer. MA: MIT Press.

Hoge, Warren. 2004. "U.S. and U.N. Are Once Again the Odd Couple Over Iraq." *The New York Times International*, November 14, p. 11.

Holland, Joshua. 2006. "The Right Wing Sets its Sights on MoveOn." Available at http://www.alternet.org/story/49935. Accessed 10/12/07.

Howard, Phillip. 2006. *New Media Campaigns and the Managed Citizen*. New York, NY: Cambridge University Press.

International Policy Studies. 2003. (www.ips-dc.org).

ivaw.org. (http://www.iraw.org) Accessed 5/16/05.

Jacobs, David. 2005. "Internet Activism and the Democratic Emergency in the United States." *Ephemera: Theory & Politics in Organization* 5(1): 68–77.

Jameson, Fredrick. 1984. "Postmodernism or the Cultural Logic of Capitalism." *New Left Review* 146: 52–92.

Jasper, James. 1997. *The Art of Moral Protest: Culture, Biography, and Creativity in Social Movements*. Chicago, IL: University of Chicago Press.

———, and Francesca Polletta. 2001. "Collective Identity and Social Movements." *American Review of Sociology* Volume 27: 283–305.

Jenkins, Henry. 2006. *Convergence Culture*. New York, NY: New York University Press.

Jenkins, Holman. 1998. "The Rise and Stumble of Nike." *Wall Street Journal*, June 3, p. A4.

Jenkins, Craig. 1983. "Resource Mobilization Theory and the Study of Social Movement. *Annual Review of Sociology* 9: 527–553.

———, and Charles Perrow. 1977. "Insurgency of the Powerless: Farm Worker Movements (1946–1972)." *American Sociological Review* 42: 249–296.

———, and William Form. 2006. "Social Movements and Social Change." pp. 331–349 in *Handbook of Political Sociology: States, Civil Society and Globalization*, edited by Thomas Janoski, Robert Alford, Alexander Hicks and Mildred Schwartz. Cambridge, MA: Cambridge University Press.

Jensen, Jeff. 1996. "Marketer of the Year: Nike." *Advertising Age*, December 30, p. A14.

Johnston, Hank. 1994. "New Social Movements and Old Regional Nationalisms. pp. 167–186 in *New Social Movements. From Ideology to Identity*, edited by

Enrique Larana, Hank Johnston and Joseph Gusfield. Philadelphia, PA: Temple University Press.
———, and Bert Klandermans. 1995. "A Methodology for Frame Analysis: From Discourse to Cognitive Schemata." pp. 217–246 in *Social Movements and Culture*. Minneapolis, MN: University of Minnesota Press.
———, and Enrique Laraña and Joseph Gusfield. 1994. *New Social Movements: From Ideology to Identity*. Philadelphia, PA: Temple University Press.
Jordan, Tim. 2001. "Measuring the Net: Host Counts Versus Business Plans." *Information, Communication and Society* 4(1): 34–53.
Kahn, Richard and Douglas Kellner. 2003. "Internet subcultures and oppositional politics." pp. 299–314 in. *The Post-subcultures Reader*, edited by David Muggleton. London, UK: Berg Publishers.
Katz, Donald. 1994. *Just Do It: The Nike Spirit in the Corporate World*. Holbrook, MA: Adams Publishers.
Katz, James and Ronald Rice. 2002. *Social Consequences of Internet Use: Access, Involvement and Expression*. Cambridge, MA: MIT Press.
Keck, Margaret and Katherine Sikkink. 1998. *Activists beyond Borders: Advocacy Networks in International Politics*. Ithaca, NY: Cornell University Press.
Kellner, Douglas. 2004. *Globalization, Technopolitics and Revolution*. pp. 180–194 in *The Future of Revolution: Rethinking Radical Change in the Age of Globalization*, edited by John Foran. New York, NY: Zed Books.
Kern, Montague. 2004. "Web and Mass Media Campaigns by Political Candidates, MoveOn.org and the Democratic Party in the 2003–04 Presidential Primaries." *School of Communication, Information and Library Studies*. Rutgers University. Available at http://sherpa.bl.uk/2/01/PMKern.html. Accessed 5/15/06.
Kershaw, Ian. 2007. "Blair Blew the 'Special Relationship." *Los Angeles Times*, May 16, p. A21.
Kidd, David. 2003. "Indymedia: A New Communications Commons." pp. 47–69 in *Cyberactivism: Online Acts in Theory and Practice*, edited by Barbara McCaughney and Michael Ayers. New York, NY: Routledge.
Kidd, Dustin. 2001. "Kukdong Update from Nike." Available at http://www.nikebize.org. Accessed 4/7/03.
Kitschelt, Herbert. 1986. "Political Opportunity Structures and Political Protest: Anti-Nuclear Movements in Four Democracies." *British Journal of Political Science* 16: 57–85.
Klandermans, Bert. 1991. "New Social Movements and Resource Mobilization: The European and the American Approach Revisited." pp. 17–44 in *Research on Social Movements: The State of the Art in Western Europe and the USA*, edited by Dieter Rucht. Frankfurt: Campus.
———. 1994. "Transient Identities? Membership Patterns in the Dutch Peace Movement." pp. 168–184 in *New Social Movements: From Ideology to Identity*, edited by Enrique Larana, Hank Johnston and Joseph Gusfiled. Philadelphia, PA: Temple University Press.
———. 1997. *The Social Psychology of Protest*. Cambridge, MA: Blackwell Publishers.
———. 2001. "Why Social Movements Come into Being and Why People Join Them." pp. 268–81 in *The Blackwell Companion to Sociology*, edited by Judith Blau. Malden, MA: Blackwell Press.
———, and Sidney Tarrow. 1988. "Mobilization into Social Movements: Synthesizing European and American Approaches." pp. 1–40 in *From Structure to Action*, edited by Bert Klandermans, Hanspeter Kriesi and Sydney Tarrow. Greenwich, CT: JAI Press.
Klein, Naomi. 2000. *No Logo*. New York, NY: Picador Press.

Kobrin, Stephen. 1998. "The Clash of Globalizations." *Foreign Policy* 112: 97–109.

Kohut, Andrew. 2008. "The Internet Gains in Politics." *Pew Internet & American Life Project*. Available at http://www.pewinternet.org/PPF/r/234/report. Accessed 10/7/09.

Kolb, Felix. 2007. *Political and Opportunities: A Theory of Social Movements and Political Change*. New York, NY: Campus Verlagg.

Kollock, Peter, and Marc Smith. 1999. *The Sociology of Cyberspace: Social Interaction and Order in Computer Communities*. Thousand Oaks, CA: Pine Forge Press.

Kornhauser, William. 1959. *The Politics of Mass Society*. Glencoe, IL: Free Press.

Korzeniewicz, Miguel. 1992. "Global Commodity Networks and the Leather Footwear Industry." *Sociology Perspectives* 35(2): 313–327.

Kraut, Robert, Michael Paterson, Sara Kiesler, Vicki Lundmark, Ridas Ukopadtyah and William Scheller. 1998. "Internet Paradox: A Social Technology that Reduces Social Involvement and Psychological Well-Being?" *American Psychologist* 53(9): 1017–1031.

Kriesi, Hanspeter. 2004. "Political Context and Opportunity." pp. 67–90 in *The Blackwell Companion to Social Movements,* edited by David Snow, Sarah Soule, Hanspeter Kriesi. Malden, MA and Oxford, UK: Blackwell Publishing.

———, and Ruud Koopmans, Jan Kuyrendak and Amark Oguign. 1995. *New Social Movements in Europe: A Comparative Analysis*. Minneapolis, MN: University of Minnesota Press.

Kuttner, Robert. 2003. "Dissent: Antiwar and Postwar, Too? You Bet." *Washington Post,* March 23, p. B02.

Laclau, Ernesto and Chantal Mouffe. 1985. *Hegemony and Social Strategy*. London, UK: Verso.

Langman, Lauren. 2005. "From Virtual Public Spheres to Global Justice: A Critical Theory of International Social Movements." *Sociological Theory* 23(1): 42–74.

Larana, Enrique. 1994. "Continuity and Unity in New Forms of Collective Action: A Comparative Analysis of Student Movements." pp. 209–233 in *New Social Movements,* edited by Enrique Larana, Hank Johnston and Joseph Gusfield. Philadelphia, PA: Temple University Press.

Lasn, Kelne. 1999. *Culture Jam: The Uncooling of Advertising*. New York, NY: Eagle Brook.

Lawrence, Jill. 2008. "Young Voters Poised to be an Election Force." *USA TODAY,* May 6, p. 1A.

Lee, Jennifer. 2003. "How Protestors Mobilized So Many and So Nimbly." *The New York Times*, February 14, p. A10.

Leland, John. 2003. "A Movement Yes, but No Counterculture." *The New York Times*, March 23, p. D7.

Liasson, Mara. 2008. "Obama Looks to Harness Grass-Roots Support." *NPR*. Available at http://www.npr.org/templates/story/story.php?storyId=96886703. Accessed 7/19/09.

Lievrouw, Leah A. and Sonia Livingstone. 2006. *Handbook of New Media: Social Shaping and Social Consequences of ICTs*. London, UK: Sage.

Liu, Ruiz, Sylvia, DeAngelo, Amy. 2009. *Findings from the 2008 Administration of the College Senior Survey (CSS): National Aggregates*. Los Angeles, CA: Higher Education Research Institute, UCLA.

Lucardie, Paul. 2000. "Prophets, Purifiers and Prolouctors: Towards a Theory on the Emergence of New Parties." *Party Politics* 6(2): 18–30.

Luo, Michael. 2007. "Antiwar Groups Use New Clout to Influence Democrats on Iraq." *The New York Times*, May 4, p. B10.

————. Lutz, Monte. 2009. SVP-Digital Public Affairs, Edelman. "The Social Pulpit: Barack Obama's Social Media Toolkit." *Edelman*. Available athttp://www.edelman.com/image/insights/content. Accessed 7/13/09.

Mann, Michael. 2000. "Has Globalization Ended the Rise of the Nation-State?" pp. 136–147 in *The Global Transformations Reader: An Introduction to the Globalization Debate*, edited by David Held and Andrew McGrew. Cambridge, MA: Polity Press.

Maquila Solidarity Network. 2001. "Nike Concedes Victory: Sportswear Giant Promises to Place Orders with Unionized Factory." December 12. Available at http://www.maqullasolidarity.org. Accessed 4/19/2003.

Markels, Alex. 2003. "Virtual Peacenik." May 5. Available at http://www.MotherJones.com/news/hellriiser/2003/05/ma_379_01.htm. Accessed 4/7.06.

Marks, Gary and Doug McAdam. 1996. "Social Movements and the Changing Structure of Political Opportunity in the European Community." pp. 95–120 in *Governance in the European Union*, edited by G. Marks, Fritz W. Scharpf, Phillipe C. Schmitter and Wolfgang Streeck. Thousand Oaks, CA: Sage.

Marullo, Sam and David Meyer. 2004. "Antiwar and Peace Movements." pp. 641–665 in *The Blackwell Companion to Social Movements*, edited by David Snow, Sarah Soule and Hanspeter Kriesi. Oxford, UK: Blackwell.

McAdam, Doug. 1982. *Political Process and the Development of Black Insurgency 1930–1970*. Chicago, IL: University of Chicago Press.

————. 1983. "Tactical Innovation and the Pace of Insurgency." *American Sociological Review* 48: 735–754.

————, and McCarthy, Zald. 1996. *Comparative Perspectives on Social Movements: Political Opportunities, Mobilizing Structures, and Cultural Framings*. New York, NY/Cambridge, MA: Cambridge University Press.

————, and Yang, Su. 2002. "The War at Home: Antiwar Protests and Congressional Voting, 1965 to 1973." *American Sociological Review* 67: 696–721.

McCarthy, John and Mayer Zald. 1973. *The Trend of Social Movements in America: Professionalization and Resource Mobilization*. Thousand Oaks, CA: General Learning Press.

————. 1977. "Resource Mobilization: A Partial Theory." *American Journal of Sociology* 82(6): 1212–1241.

————. 1987. Social Movements in an Organizational Society. New Brunswick, NJ: Transaction Books.

McCaughney, Martha and Michael Ayers. 2003. *Cyberactivism: Online Activism in Theory and Practice*. New York, NY: Routledge.

McCammon, Holly J., Karen E. Campbell, Ellen M. Granberg and Christine Mowery. 2001. "How Movements Win: Gendered Opportunity Structures and the State Women's Suffrage Movements, 1866–1919." *American Sociological Review* 66: 49–70.

McDonald, K. 2002. "From Solidarity to Fluidarity: Social Movements Beyond Collective Identity." *Social Movement Studies* 1(2): 109–128.

McGinnis, Joe. 1988. *The Selling of the President*. New York, NY: Penguin.

Meikle, Graham. 2002. *Future Active: Media Access and the Internet*. New York, NY: Routledge.

Melber, Ari. 2007. "The Virtual Primary." *The Nation*, July 7, p. 30.

Melucci, Alberto. 1980. "The New Social Movements: A Theoretical Approach." *Social Science Information* 19: 199–226.

————. 1985. "The Symbolic Challenge of Contemporary Movements." *Social Research* 52: 789–816.

————. 1989. *Nomads of the Present*. London, UK: Hutchinson Radius.

————. 1996. *Challenging Codes of Collective Action in the Information Age*. Cambridge, MA: Cambridge University Press.

Meyer, David S. 2005. "Introduction: Social Movements and Public Policy: Eggs, Chicken, and Theory." Introduction in *Routing the Opposition: Social Movements, Public Policy and Democracy,* edited by David S. Meyers, Valerie Jenness and Helen Ingram. Minneapolis, MN: University of Minnesota Press.

———. 2006. *The Politics of Protest: Social Movements in America.* New York, NY: Oxford University Press.

———, and Debra Minkoff. 2004. "Conceptualizing political opportunity." *Social Force* 82(4): 1457–1492.

———, and Suzanne Staggenborg. 1996. "Movements, Countermovements, and the Structure of Political Opportunity." *American Journal of Sociology* 101(6): 1628–1660.

———, and Suzanne Staggenborg. 1998. "Countermovement Dynamics in Federal Systems: A comparison of Abortion Politics in Canada and the United States." Research in Political Sociology 8: 209–240.

Middleton, Joel and Donald Green. 2007. "Do Community-Based Voter Mobilization Campaigns Work Even in Battleground States? Evaluating the Effectiveness of MoveOn's 2004 Outreach Campaign." *Yale University.* Available at www.yale.edu/csaps/seminars/middleton.pdf. Accessed 1/19/09.

Minkoff, Debra. 1997. "The Sequencing of Social Movements." *American Sociological Review* 62: 779–799.

Milstein, Cindy. 2003. "Recovering the Power of the Global Grass Roots in the Antiwar Movement."Available at www.social-ecology.org/learn/library. Accessed 4/2/05.

Moberg, David. 1997. "Just Do It: Inside Nike's New Age Sweatshops." *Los Angeles Weekly,* June 19, p. 17.

Morris, Aldon. 1984. *The Origins of the Civil Rights Movement: Black Communities Organizing for Change.* New York, NY: Free Press.

Morrison, Denton E. 1978. "Some Notes toward Theory on Relative Deprivation, Social Movements, and Social Change." pp. 202–209 in *Collective Behavior and Social Movements,* edited by Louis E. Genevie. Itasca, IL: Peacock.

Mouffe, Chantal. 1992. *Dimensions of Radical Democracy: Pluralism, Citizenship, Community.* London, UK/New York, NY: Verso.

MoveOn.org. 2004. "Statement." Available at http://www.moveonpac.org/whoweare.html. Accessed 4/6008.

———. 2005. Available at http://www.moveon.org/006report.

———. 2006. "Election 2006: People-Powered Politics." Available at http://www.moveon.org. Accessed 4/6/08.

———. 2008. "People-Powered Politics." Available at http://www.moveon.org. Accessed 12/30/08.

Mueller, Carol. 1994. "Conflict Networks and the Origins of Women's Liberation." pp. 234–263 in *New Social Movements,* edited by Enrique Larana, Hank Johnston and Joseph Gusfield. Philadelphia, PA: Temple University Press.

New York Times. 2002. "MoveOn Paid advertisement." December 11, p. 12.

———. 2003. "Artists United to Win Without War paid advertisement." February 15, p. 9.

Nie, Norman. 2001. "Sociability, Interpersonal Relations and the Internet." *American Behavioral Scientist* 45(3): 420–435.

———, and Lutz Erbring. 2000. "Internet and Society." *Stanford Institute for the Quantitative Study of Society.* Available http://www.stanford.edu/groups/siqss/Press_Release/Preliminary_Report.pdf. Accessed 4/7/02.

Nielsen Media Report. 2007. Available at http://www.neilsen.com/nielsenwire/media. Accessed 12/10/09.

Nieves, Evelyn. 2003. "Antiwar Groups Say Public Ire Over Iraq Claims Is Increasing." *Washington Post,* July 22, p. A03.

Nightline. 1996. June 16.

Nike Annual Report. 1996. Available at http://nikebiz.com. Accessed 7/10/07.

Nipp, Joyce. 2004. "The Queer Sisters and its Electronic Bulletin Board: A Study of the Internet for Social Movement Mobilization." pp. 233–258 in *Cyberprotest: New Media, Citizens and Social Movements,* edited by Wim Van De Donk, Brian Loader, Paul Nixon and Dieter Ructh. New York, NY: Routledge.

Oberschall, Anthony. 1973. *Social Conflict and Social Movements.* Englewood Cliffs, NJ: Prentice Hall.

Offe, Claus. 1985. "New Social Movements: Changing Boundaries of the Political." *Social Research* 52: 817–868.

Olson, Mancur. 1971. *The Logic of Collective Action: Public Goods and the Theory of Groups.* Cambridge, MA: Harvard University Press.

Organizing for America. 2007. "Obama Campaign to Launch Generation Obama." *BarackObama.com.* Available at http://www.barackobama.com/2007/08/22/obama_campaign. Accessed 5/9/08.

Owens, William. 2006. *Lifting the Fog of War.* Baltimore, MD: Johns Hopkins University Press.

Packer, George. 2003. "Part of the Success of the Feb. 15 Demonstrations, and of the Movement Itself, Lies in the Simplicity of the Message." *New York Times Magazine,* pp. 8–9.

Peaceful Tomorrows.org. Available at http://www.peacfultomorrows.org. Accessed 2/10/05.

Peretti, Jonhah. 2001. "My Nike Media Adventure." *The Nation,* April 9, pp. 22–24.

Peter, Tom. 2007. "National Intelligence Estimate: Al Qaeda Stronger and a Threat to US Homeland." *The Christian Science Monitor,* July 19, pp. 22–26.

PEW Research Center. 2003. Available at http://pewresearch.org/pubs/432. Accessed 7/3/05.

Pickerill, Jenny. 2003. *Cyberprotest: Environmental Activism.* New York, NY: Manchester University Press.

PIPA (Program on International Policy Attitudes). 1999. "Americans on Globalization: A Study of U.S. Public Attitudes." Available at http://www.pipa.org/onlinereprts/globalization_html. Accessed 7/6/02.

Piven, Frances and Richard Cloward. 1977. *Poor People's Movements: Why They Succeed, Why They Fail.* New York, NY: Pantheon Books.

Pliskin, Nova and Cella T. Romm. 1997. "The Impact of e-mail on the Evolution of a Virtual Community During a Strike." *Information & Management* 32: 245–254.

Polletta, Francesca. 2008. "Culture and Movements." *The Annals of the American Academy of Political and Social Science* 6(1): 78–96.

———. James M. Jasper. 2001. "Collective Identity and Social Movements." *Annual Review of Sociology* 27: 283–305.

Poster, Mark. 1995. *Second Media Age.* Cambridge, MA: Polity Press.

Potter, Trevor. 2003. "Internet Politics 2000: Over-hyped, then Under-hyped, the Revolution Begins." *Election Law Journal* 1(1): 25–33.

Pough, Tony. 2001. "Against Tide, They Clamor For Peace." *The Philadelphia Inquirer,* September 21, p. 16.

Press for Change. Available at http://www.pressforchange.org. Accessed 4/1/03.

Putnam, Robert. 2000. *Bowling Alone: The Collapse and Renewal of American Community.* New York, NY: Simon and Schuster.

Rainie, Lee, John Horrigan and Michael Cornfield. 2005. "The Internet and Campaign 2004." *Pew Internet & American Life* Project. Available at http://www.pewinternet.org/Reports/2005/The-Internet-and-Campaign-2004.aspx. Accessed 10/12/08.

Rao, Niva. 1997. "Networks Form to cut Pakistani Child Labor." *Journal of Commerce*, p. 4.

Reilly, Adam. 2004. "MoveOn Confronts the Future. How Does a Grassroots Power Redirect its Muscle?" Available at http://www.boston/news_features/otherstories/04302654.asp. Accessed 7/9/06.

Rheingold, Howard. 2002. *Smart Mobs: The Next Social Revolution*. Cambridge, MA: Basic Books.

———. 2003. *Smart Mobs: The Next Social Revolution. Part 3*. Cambridge, MA: Basic Books.

Rice, Alexis. 2003. "The Use of Blogs in the 2004 Presidential Election." Available at http://www.campaignsonline.org//reports/blog.pdf. Accessed 7/8/05.

Ripley, Neil. 2008. "What Happened to the Coalition of the Willing?" Available at http://www.watchdog.org. Accessed 4/7/09.

Rojas, H. 2006. Comunicación, Participación y Democracia. Universitas Humanistica 62: 109–142.

Rooney, Megan. 2003. "Pleas for Peace, Then and Now."*Chronicle of Higher Education* 49(30):A8.

Ross, Andrew. 1999. *No Sweat*. New York, NY: Verso Press.

Ross, John. 2004. "Bush Tells the World to Drop Dead." Available athttp://www.counterpunch.org/ross03272004.html. Accessed 4/7/05.

Rucht, Dieter. 1988. "Themes, Logics, and Arenas of Social Movements: A Structural Approach." *International Social Movement Research* 1: 305–328.

Ruffini, Patrick. 2008. "How Revolutionary is Obama´s Anti-FISA Group?" *The Next Right*. Available at http://www.thenextright.com/patrick-ruffini/how-revolutionary-obamas-anti-fisa-group. Accessed 9/8/09.

Ryan, Charlotte and William A. Gamson. 2006. "The Art of Reframing Political Debates" *Contexts* 5(1): 13–18.

Santana, Rebecca. 2009. "Twittering the Electoral Crisis in Iran. Available at http://www.usatoday.com. Accessed 3/10/10.

Santoro, Wayne. 2002. "The Civil Rights Movements' Struggle for Fair Employment: A 'Dramatic Events—Conventional Politics' Model." *Social Forces* 81: 177–206.

Scahill, Jeremy. 2004. "The New York Model: Indymedia and the Text Message Jihad." *ZNet*, September 9, p. 16.

Schanberg, Sindey. 1996. "Six Cents an Hour." *Life Magazine*, June, pp. 38–48.

Schraeder, Jordan. 2002. "Sweatshop Worker Credits University of Michigan for Better Working Conditions." *Michigan Daily*, December 4, p. D20.

SGMA. 1999. "Footwear Marketing Insights." Florida: SGMA.

Shaw, Randy. 1999. *Reclaiming America*. Berkeley, CA: University of California Press.

Sifry, Micah. 2008. "The FISA Protest and MyBO: Can We Talk? Can They Listen?" Available at http://techpresident.com/blog-entry/fisa-protest-and-mybo-can-we-talk-can-they-listen. Accessed 7/9/09.

Sikkink, Kathyrn. 2005. "Patterns of Dynamic Multilevel Governance and the Insider–Outsider Coalition." pp. 204–237 in *Transnational Protest and Global Activism: People, Passions, and Power*, edited by Donatella Della Porta and Sidney Tarrow. Lanham, MD: Rowman and Littlefield.

Singel, Ryan. 2004. "Net Politics Down but Not Out." *Wired*, February 2. Available at http://www.wired.com/politics/law/news/2004/02/62123. Accessed 7/7/06.

Sklair, Leslie. 1998. "The Transnational Capitalist Class and Global Capitalism." *Political Power and Social Theory* 12: 3–43.

Smelser, Neil J. 1962. *Theory of Collective Behavior*. New York, NY: The Free Press.

Smith, Aaron. 2009. "The Internet's Role in Campaign 2008." *PEW Internet and American Life Project*. Available at http://www.pewinternet.org/Reports/2009/6—The-Internets-Role-in-Campaign-2008.aspx. Accessed 12/18/09.

———, and Lee Rainie. 2008. "The Internet and the 2008 Election." *Pew Internet & American Life Project. Available at* http://pewinternet.org/Reports/2008/The-Internet-and-the-2008-Election.aspx. Accessed 12/18/09.

Smith, Jackie. 2002. "Bridging Global Divides? Strategic Framing and Solidarity in Transnational Social Movement Organizations." *International Sociology* 17(4): 505–528.

Smith, Jackie and Hank Johnston. 2002. "Globalization and Resistance: An Introduction." pp. 112 in *Transnational Dimensions of Social Movements*, edited by Hank Johnston and Jackie Smith.Lanham, MD: Rowman and Littlefield.

Snow, David A. Burke Rochford, Steven K. Worden, Robert D. Benford. 1986. "Frame Alignment Processes, Micromobilization, and Movement Participation." *American Sociological Review* 51: 464–481.

———, and Doug McAdam. 2000. "Identity Work Processes in the Context of Social Movements." pp. 41–67 in *Self, Identity and Social Movements*, edited by Sheldon Stryker, Timothy J. Owens and Robert White. University of Minnesota Press.

———, and Robert Benford. 1992. "Master Frames and Cycles of Protest." pp. 133–156 in *Frontiers in Social Movement Theory*, edited by Aldon Morris and Carol McClurg Mueller. New Haven, CT: Yale University Press.

Solomon, Mark. 2004. "What Next? Let's Build The Mother Of All Coalitions." Available at http://www.portside@lists.portside.org. Accessed 1/9/06.

Soule, Sarah. 2004. "Going to the Chapel? Same-Sex Marriage Bans in the United States, 1973–2000." *Social Problems* 51(4): 453–477.

———, and Brayden King. 2006. "The Stages of the Policy Process and the Equal Rights Amendment, 1972–1982." *American Journal of Sociology* 111(6): 1871–1909.

———, and Brayden G. King. 2008. "Competition and resource partitioning in three social movement industries." *American Journal of Sociology* 113(6): 1568–1610.

———, and Douglas McAdam, John McCarthy and Y. Su. 1999. "Protests Events: Cause or Consequence of the U.S. women's movement and federal congressional activities, 1956–1979." *Mobilization* 4(2): 239–256.

———, and Jennifer Earl. 2005. "A Movement Society Evaluated: Collective Protest in the United States 1960–1986. *Mobilization* 10(3): 345–364.

———, and Susan Olzak. 2004. "When Do Social Movements Matter? The Politics of Contingency and the Equal Rights Amendment, 1972–1982." American Sociological Review 69: 473–497.

Staggenborg, Suzanne. 1988. "The Consequences of Professionalization and Formalization in the Pro-Choice Movement" *American Sociological Review* 53: 585–606.

Stauber, John. 2010. "Tea Party Money-Bomb Elects Scott Brown, Blows-Up Obamacare." Available at http://www.prwatch.org/node/8841. Accessed 3/1/2010.

Stelter, Brian. 2008. "The Facebooker Who Friended Obama." *New York Times*, July 7, p. E4.

Stengel, Richard. 2001. "The First Internet War." *Time Magazine,* October 25, p. 22.

Sternberg, Andy. 2008. October 28. "Obama Facebook App Targets Your Friends in Battleground States." *NetZoo*. Available at http://netzero.net.obama-facebook-app-targets-your-friends-in-battleground-states/. Accessed 10/10/09.

Stevenson, Richard. 2003. "Bush: Ten Million People is a 'Focus group'." *New York Times*, February 19, A4.

Stevenson, Seth. 2004. "Not-So-Amateur Night." *Slate Magazine*, January 13, p. 27.

Stewart, Ian. 2003. "Anti-War Group Revives 'Daisy' Ad Campaign." *Common Dreams*. Available at http://www.commondreams.org/headlines03/0116-06. htm. Accessed 9/4/04.

Suh, Doowon. 2001. "How Do Political Opportunities Matter for Social Movements?: Political Opportunity, Misframing, Pseudosucess and Pseudofailure." *The Sociological Quarterly* 42(3): 437–460.

Swp.org. 2005. "A Cycle of War and Despair." July 13, p. 23. Available at http://www.swp.org.uk/aftermath.php. Accessed 6/9/07.

Tarrow, Sidney. 1988."The Oldest New Movement." pp. 281304 in *From Structure to Action: Comparing Social Movements Across Cultures*, edited by Bert Klandermans, Hanspeter Kriesi and Sidney Tarrow, International Social Movement Research I. Greenwich, CT: JAI.

1991. "Struggle, Politics, and Reform: Collective Action, Social Movements, and Cycles of Protest." *Western Societies Program,* Occasional paper no. 21, Center for International Studies. Ithaca, NY: Cornell University Press.

———. 1994. *Power in Movement. Social Movements, Collective Action and Politics.* Cambridge, MA; Cambridge University Press.

———. 1996. "States and Opportunities: The Political Structuring of Social Movements." pp. 41–47 in *Comparative Perspectives in Social Movements,* edited by Doug McAdam, John D. McCarthy and Mayer N. Zald. New York, NY: Cambridge University Press.

———. 1998. *Power in Movement: Social Movements and Contentious Politics,* 2nd ed., Cambridge, MA: Cambridge University Press.

———. 2001. "Transnational Politics." *Annual Review of Political Science* 4(1): 1–20.

———, and Charles Tilly. 2006. *Contentious Politics.* Boulder, CO: Paradigm Publishers

Taylor, Verta and Nella Van Dyke. 2004. "Get Up, Stand Up: Tactical Repertoires of Social Movements." pp. 262–293 in The *Blackwell Companion to Social Movements Reader,* edited by David Snow, Sarah Sole and Henrik Kriesi. Oxford, UK: Blackwell Publishers.

Thao, Hua. 1996. "Nike Protestor Charges Abuse of Employee Labor." *Los Angeles Times,* December, p. D7.

Tilly, Charles. 1973. "Do Communities Act?" *Sociological Inquiry* 43: 3–4.

———. 1978. *From Mobilization to Revolution.* Reading, MA: Addison-Wesley.

———. 2001. *Dynamics of Contention.* Cambridge, MA: Cambridge University Press.

———. 2004. *Social Movements.* Boulder, CO: Paradigm Publishers.

———. 2006. *Regimes and Repertoires.* Chicago, IL: University of Chicago Press.

Times, The. 2007. "Spain Furious as US Blocks Access to Madrid Bombing." February 15, p. 18.

Tisch, Jonathan. 2008. "Youth Turnout." *The Center for Information & Research on Civic Learning and Engagement.* Available at http://www.civicyouth.org/index.php?s=Jonathan+Tisch). Accessed 5/17/09.

Tomilinson, John. 2002. *Globalization and Culture.* Chicago, IL: University of Chicago Press.

Touraine, Alain. 1985. "An Introduction to the Study of Social Movements." *Social Research* 52(4): 749–788.

United Students Against Sweatshops. Available at usas@yahoogroups.com. Accessed 10/8/04.

Utne, Leif. 2003. "MoveOn.org Holds Virtual Primary." June 23. Available at http://www.utune.com/webwatch/2003_731/news/10655-1.html. Accessed 9/9/08.

Van Aelst, Peter. 2002. "New Media, New Movements? The Role of the Internet in Shaping the 'Anti-Globalization' Movement." In *Cyberprotest: New Media, Citizens and Social Movement*, edited by William van de Donk, Brian D. Loader, Paul G. Nixon & Dieter Rucht. London, Routledge, pp. 229–254.

———, and Stephaan Walgrave. 2003. "Open and Closed Mobilization Contexts and the Normalization of the Protester." pp. 123–146 in *Cyberprotest: New Media, and Citizen Social Movements*, edited by Wim Van De Donk, Brian Lad, Paul Nixon and Dieter Ructh. London, UK: Routledge.

Vargas, Jose Antonio. 2008. "Obama Raised Half a Billion Online." *The Washington Post*. Available at http://voices.washingtonpost.com/44/2008/11/20/obama_raised_half_billion_on.html. Accessed 4/9/09.

Webb, Cynthia. 2003. "Overseas, Internet Is Rallying Point for Antiwar Activists." *Washington Post*, March 12, p. 4.

Wellman, Barry. 2002. "Changing Connectivity: A Future History of Y2.03K." *Sociological Research Online* 4(4). Available at http://www.socresonline.org.uk/4/4/wellman.html.

Whitehouse.gov. Available at http://www.whitehouse.gov/news/release/2007/05/print/20070524.html. Accessed 4/19/07.

Whitney, Daisy. 2007. "ABC News Partners with Facebook on 2008 Elections." Available at htto://www.tvweek.com/news/2007/11/abc_news_partners_with_facebook.php. Accessed 4/5/09.

WhyWar?.org. Available at http://www.whywar.org. Accessed 9/3/04.

Williams, Rhys H. 2004. "The Cultural Contexts of Collective Action: Constraints, Opportunities, and the Symbolic Life of Social Movements." pp. 91–115 in *The Blackwell Companion to Social Movements*, edited by David Snow, Sarah Soule and Hanspeter Kriesi. Malden, MA and Oxford, UK: Blackwell Publishing.

WinWithoutWar.org. Available at http://winwithoutwar.org. Accessed 10/8/06.

Wolf, Gary. 2004. "How the Internet Invented Howard Dean." *Wired*, January. Available at http://www.wired.com/wired/archive/12.01/dean.html. Accessed 5/17/05.

Wright, John. 1996. *Interest Groups and Congress*. Boston, MA: Allyn and Bacon.

Wuthnow, R.1998. *Loose Connections: Joining Together in America's Fragmented Communities*. Cambridge, MA: Harvard University Press.

Zachary, Coile and Marc Sandalow.2004. "Observers See Eerie Parallels in Attacks on Kerry, McCain." *San Francisco Chronicle*, August 24, p. B21.

Zald, Mayer N. 1996. "Culture Ideology and Strategic Framing." In *Comparative Perspectives in Social Movements*, edited by Doug McAdam, John D. McCarthy, Mayer N. Zald. Cambridge, MA: Cambridge University Press.

Index